1857 IN NORTH EAST:

A RECONSTRUCTION FROM FOLK AND ORAL SOURCES

1857 IN NORTH EAST

A RECONSTRUCTION FROM FOLK AND ORAL SOURCES

Subir Kar
Professor, Department of Bengali
Assam University, Silchar

AKANSHA PUBLISHING HOUSE
NEW DELHI - 110 002 (INDIA)

AKANSHA PUBLISHING HOUSE
4649/21-B, Ansari Road
Daryaganj, New Delhi - 110 002
Phones: 23263193, 9811582579, 9435116718
E-mail: ektabooks@yahoo.com

1857 in North East: A Reconstruction from Folk and Oral Sources

First Published, 2008

ISBN-978-81-8370-131-0

PRINTED IN INDIA

Published by Akansha Publishing House, New Delhi-110 002
and Printed at Aryan Enterprises, Delhi

Dedicated to

Rita Kar

Contents

Preface

The hundred and fifty years of 1857 is calling at the door. The slogan 'to us belong our Hindustan, to none else' is still reverberating I feel it is the right time to 'Hail and Salute' the Martyrs who sacrificed their lives for the noble cause of the country and share with the readers, the sagas of our ancestors, who might not have taken arms in their hands but heartily believed that the uprise was for the freedom and the failure was the great tragedy of the nation. Like other parts of the Country like Brij area of Meerut, Bhojpur of Bihar, Oudh, Jhansi, Gujarat, Rajasthan, Delhi etc., the common people of the North-East Region who mainly belonged to the fishermen community and peasantry, composed innumerable songs and ballads on the historical incidents of the great Mutiny 1857. Till today these are recited in groups and individually sung by the bards in mass gatherings. Besides these folk songs and the ballads on the great Rebellion, the mass also sing the songs composed on the Revolt of Nawab Radharam, Maniram Dewan, Bir Sambhudhan who sacrificed their lives in the struggles against the British Regime. The people of the tea garden areas of Assam, till today, sing the popular songs of the heroic tales on Kunwar Singh, the great father of Bhojpur.

The most popular ballad *'Jangiyar geet'*,— the songs of the warriors, constitute a very valuable source material in formulating appropriate history of our glorious past. The revolt of the 34th Native Infantry Regiment at Chittagong, on November 18, 1857, as a sequel to the great Sepoy Mutiny, and its follow up actions and reactions that occurred throughout the entire region from Chittagong, Sylhet (now in Bangladesh), and the areas of the present district of Karimganj, Hailakandi and Cachar, Assam, has been narrated in detail in the folk ballad. This was recorded at the period of field survey in the month of December, 1979, from the mouth of an octogenarian village bard Haji Md. Asfar Ali, son of late Motor Ali Shah of the village Inat Pur, three kilometers away from Karimganj town and hardly five kilometers from Latu Bazar, where a fierce fight took place between the Mutineers and the Sylhet Light Infantry on December 19, 1857.

This ballad is a complete episode with a regular sequence of events beginning with a convincing cause which stirred the sentiment of the common people to rise and stand united against the oppressions and cruelty of the British regime.

All these events recall the glorious history of the brave people who sacrificed their lives for their motherland during the period of 'the War of freedom 1857'.

I felt attracted to this folk-ballad and the tales and songs for many reasons. Firstly, a few stray songs sung by passersby on the street and river sides enchanted my mind from my early boyhood. Secondly, the pitched battle that took place at Latu between the mutineers of 1857 and Sylhet Light Infantry, and the route the fugitives followed in all these areas are closely associated with me as I personally belong to this region. And the common people commemorate the incidents and orally transmit it to the next generation which they have acquired from their ancestors. Later, I started collecting historical data and documents which threw light on the mutiny the relevance of which is well associated with the incidents referred to in the folk-ballad. In spite of my earnest zeal to go into the subject the paucity of relevant books and concerned materials prevented me to undertake any project.

After a lapse of several years, in 1984, the persuasion of Dr. Sukumar Biswas, Professor and Head of Bengali Department, Gauhati University inspired me to take up the subject afresh. In the mean time, the book 'Mutiny Period in Cachar' came in my hand as a treasure of source material for the historical data. This book has been compiled and edited by Dr. Sujit Choudhury and published by the Tagore Society for Cultural Integration, Silchar, in 1981. From the editorial notes of Mr. H. Gupta and Mr. S. Choudhury it is learnt that the manuscript of this book belonged to Mr. Taramani Choudhury a friend of Robert Reid of England. James Reid, the father of William Reid and Robert Reid, in the early years of twentieth Century, came to Cachar and worked as Tea garden Manager. During the period of his stay in Cachar he married one Bengali Muslim lady. William Reid and Robert Reid are offspring of that union. After the death of Taramani Choudhury this manuscript was taken into the custody of Mr. A.F. Golam Osmani. Later on Mr. Osmani handed over this compilation of documents to the Tagore Society for publication.

This book contains the valuable notes and correspondences of R. Stewart, who was the Superintendent of Cachar during the eventful days of the great Mutiny 1857-58. Some letters of R. Stewart on the relevant incidents are also made available in the District Record office in Cachar. Other than these, District Gazetteers and several other books, records, documents and accounts preserved in National Archives, National Library, State Archives etc. were consulted and ultimately it was realized that these folk songs and the ballads are the part of our rich national heritage. The emotion and the aspiration of the people, the heroic spirit coupled with a feeling of patriotism and religious and social solidarity and the heroic march of the rebellious group in order to wipe out the foreign authority from the country are indeed the prime theme of this folk-ballad the *'Jangiyar Geet'* as it is popularly known in the region of Surma (now in Bangladesh) and Barak Valley in Assam. Sri Jayanta Bhushan Bhattacharjee Professor and the former Vice-Chancellor of Assam University, Silchar, mentioned excerpts of such three songs,which were collected from the mouth of one Janmejoy Barman, a scion of the Royal clan, that contain contents bearing on the Sepoy Mutiny.

There in the village Mohanpur of Hailakandi district, the rural people, specially an octogenarian muslim professional folk -bard sings the episode of the *'Jangir Larai'*, 'the War of the Rebellious', the prime theme and the object of which is also the Mutiny 1857. In the hills and valleys of Bhuban, Jalenga, Binna Kandi, Sares Pur, the people till today sing stray songs and commemorate the incidents which occurred during the period of struggle between the fugitive mutineers and the British soldiers.

The characters and personalities narrated in the ballad and the local geographical account available in the verses are real one. The picture of the agricultural land, the marshy swamps valley, impenetrable hills and jungles, rivers, purity of love and affections, role of the common people,the role of the cruel autocratic and arbitrary nature of the men in power and prestige, — all have been portrayed in an authentic realistic value in this narrative. The Geet emphasizes more on the attitude towards the confrontation and sufferings of the life that emerged from a serious socio-religious and political problems of Indian National history.

All these songs and tales definitely provide us with the fact that the people of the region observed closely the activities of the mutineers and heartily shared the cause for which the warriors dedicated their lives.

Other than these in the Valley of Brahmaputra the people still remember the sacrifice of Dewan Maniram who was hanged in the mutiny period 1857, and sing the popular folk songs on these incidents composed by the unknown village bards.

There are also many such folk- songs composed on the historical events of confrontation and struggles with the independent king of Jayantia and the British before and after Mutiny of 1857. The revolt of Sambhudhan of North Cachar in 1881-1882 is also commemorated by the tribes of the region in folk songs saluting the incidents.

The preservation of these songs and ballads in the folk-minds through ages determined the fact that, the sentiments and the imaginative vision of heroism were aroused by the events of the bygone days, a living experience of the people passed into the pages of history, and the living memory of the people came down through their folk-traditions.

The unwritten literature, composed in the form of local Bengali dialectical character, handed down through oral traditions has been reproduced in narrative form in the relevant chapter of the book.

I am indebted to Professor Sajal Nag and Dr Suryasikha Pathak, department of History, Assam University, for their persuasion and encouragement.

I am also indebted to Sanjib Deb Laskar who voluntarily came forward to translate the folk songs of the ballad from its original Bengali dialectical form into English. My affectionate niece Debasree and my Research scholar Sri Ramakanta Das, Lecturer, Radhamadhab College, Silchar, who helped me in computer works time to time deserve my heartfelt thanks.

At last I recall my sweet memories of those days when my life-partner Mrs Rita Kar who with her joyful heart shared all troubles in copying the entire episode recorded in the cassettes, in written form overcoming all her serious illness and rendered relentless services towards the completion of my Ph.D. works. In this moment her loss is felt ever more deeply.

—Subik Kar

"QAUMI TARANA"

The Flag Song 1857

"To us belongs our Hindustan
and to none else
Our sacred motherland
dearer than Heaven
The world is aglow
with the light of her soul.

How old, how new
and unique of its kind
To us belongs our Hindustan
and to none else.

Ganga and Jamuna making
our lands fertile
And overhead the snow-clad mountain
Our sentry towering
Beating against the coasts below
the trumpets of the seas.

And gold and diamonds from our mines
Over flow.
Our pomp and splendour evoking the
envy of the world..
And then came the Firangi
and such magic spell he cast.
Pillaging and plundering our motherland

He ruled.

The martyrs call you, O countrymen
do you hear?
Smash up the chains of slavery
and pour out fire
Hindus and Muslims and Sikhs –
all of us brothers.
Hail and salute it,
Here is our flag of freedom!

[It was first published in the contemporary, Payami Azadi, whose original is reported to be in the British Museum. This song is quoted from P.C. Joshi's book '1857 IN FOLK SONGS'.]

1

Mutiny Period in North East: An Overview

All the renowned historians, who have written and reviewed the history of the Sepoy Mutiny, 1857, have not given detailed account of the outbreak of Dacca and Chittagong uprisings and its impact on the North East Region of the country specially Surma-Barak Valley. Ramesh Chandra Majumdar writes, "Bengal was practically unaffected by the Mutiny with the exception of two sporadic outbursts at Dacca Chittagong. On November 18, the 34th N.I. at Chittagong mutinied and followed usual procedure. They found no sympathy among the people and, being defeated by the loyal Native Regiment, marched northwards through Sylhet and Cachar. Being defeated they turned towards the east and were joined by some discontented chiefs of Manipur living in Cachar. But they could not enter Manipur whose ruler, at the request of the British, sent his troops and captured a number of them. They were handed over to the British and the rest betook themselves to the neighbouring hills and jungles."[1]

E.A. Gait stated, "The great Sepoy Mutiny of 1857 left Assam almost untouched. The situation was at times by no means free from danger; and the comparative immunity which this part of India enjoyed was due very largely to the watchfulness and recourse displayed by the civil and military officers on the spot. Shortly before the first outbreak Mr. Allen of the Board of Revenue, had been deputed to visit the Khasi and Jaintia Hills and the Lieutenant Governor, Sir Fredrick Halliday took advantage of his presence at Cherrapunji, then the capital of that district, to place him temporarily in charge of the Eastern Frontier, including Sylhet and Cachar. Exaggerated stories of the fall of the British power caused some excitement amongst the Khasi chiefs, and the ex-Raja of Jaintia began to intrigue with some of them with a view to the recovery of his lost possession. Mr. Allen thought that to cause his arrest would invest the matter with undue importance. He therefore contented himself with ordering him to reside in Sylhet town, where he would be under the eye of the British authorities".[2] Gait's statement that the mutiny 'left Assam untouched' is simply a recorded official version of the British historian.

R.C. Mazumdar's statement regarding the revolt of 34th Native Infantry Regiment that it was a 'sporadic' outburst, and the view of the historians that 'they found no sympathy among the people', all these opinions are the reproduction of the contemporary acconts of the British officials and the historians. In fact the colonial agression of the East India Company, their land-hungry character and unbounded greed and business motive all these attitudes made the people both of the plains and hills hostile towards the foreign intruders. Behind the policy of annexation of the tribal areas of North East, how far the commercial motive of the British was effective that can easily be assessed from the following report; "There is much reason to believe that the country is rich in many natural products. Its cotton trade has always been considerable, and the Lieutenant Governor hopes that instead of our having to burn large quantities of cotton in punishment of outrage, as was unhappily necessary in a few instances, we may find here a new source of supply to Manchester. The Deputy Commissioner is now doing what he can, by the introduction of improved seed and by encouraging trade, to develop this cultivation. The timber of the hills is also expected to prove valuable, and, ... Government may expect a fair return from judicious forest operations. Wild elephants are said to be very numerous, and probably *Khedda* (trap for capturing wild elephants) operations would prove profitable at an early date."[3]

Let us now look into the entire political scenario of the North-East Region except Surma-Barak Valley, which includes the districts of Sylhet and Cachar, and its impact on the people of the region under British since its annexation up to the period of the great Mutiny 1857.

On the day of February 24, 1826, the Treaty of Yandabo was signed and Assam came under the rule of the British. In the treaty, His Majesty the King of Ava, renounced his all claims upon 'the principality of Assam and its dependencies'. The Burmese also had to withdraw their possession in the neighboring states of Manipur, Cachar and Jayantia. "At this present (moment) the growl of tiger is every where heard; as many as thirteen (to) fifteen (thousand) Europeans have been destroyed. There is no account of their numbers. In the west all the gardens are destroyed and the owner of them together with (their) wives and children have been destroyed beyond calculation...the few that escape, the mad dog devours by the way. The old hunters are extinct; if news have been sent for new hunters to come, till the tigers are so numerous, how many can the hunters kill? To escape the present calamity, many say, will be difficult; and the place where you reside, the owners are in great fear when they may decamp, there is no knowing. At the moment this occurs, you having kept your ears open, must stand up; and the forces there you must bring over to your side by means of gold and by persuasion, by any and every means in your power...agree to augment their pay in future; without doubt good must follow.[4]

This letter was written by the hero of the Mutiny, Maniram Dewan, to Maheedhur Sarma, a Mooktear of Jorhat, Assam. At the period of mutiny Assam was not far away from the revolt. The deprived and disgraced King and his kinsmen and other nobilities of Assam who ruled over the vast territory in Brahmaputra valley for more than six centuries were very much aggrieved with the policy of the foreign rule. "To persue schemes of conquest and extension of dominion in India are measures repugnant to the wish, honour and policy of this nation"; - that was the declaration of the British authority in England. After the Burmese war George Swinton, the Agent to the Governor General, North-East Frontier and the Political Secretary to the Government of India, reaffirmed the position by a statement that,' although by our expulsion of the Burmese from the territory of Assam, the country would of right become ours by conquest, the Governor General in Council does not contemplate the parmanent annexation of any part of it to the British dominion'. David Scott, the Agent to the Governor General, North-East Frontier, just before the march of his troops into Assam, in a proclamation, addressed the people of Assam by the following words, "The wished for opportunity of relieving you from the hands of your oppression has now arrived. Our victorious army has crossed the boundary and ere long we will derive the barbarians beyond the Burmahkund nor cease to destroy them until we restore peace and security to your distracted country. Come forward, therefore, without fear for the present or for the future... We further declare that we are not led into your country by the thirst of conquest; but are forced in our defence to deprive our enemy of the means of annoying us. You may therefore rest assured that we will never consent to depart until we exclude our foe from Assam and re-establish in that country a Government adopted to your wants and calculated to promote the happiness of the people of all classes."[5]

But very soon the attitude of the shrewd British power came out with its ulterior motive of colonization of Assam, 'to promote the happiness' of their own.

Narrating the contemporary incidents H.K. Barpujari states, "Of the fugitive princes of Upper Assam, after the capitulation of Rangpur, Jogeswar Singha settled himself at Jogighopa, on the north of Goalpara where he died in 1825. Chandra Kanta Singha, on account of his intriguing nature, was removed to Kaliabar in Central Assam. He was given a pension of Rupees two hundred besides one hundred pykes and rent- free grants. Purandar Singha returned to Gauhati; no allowance was made in his favour, he was reported to have then considerable wealth in his possession. Pecuniary assistance and rent-free grants were made to several members of the royal family." It is interesting to note that on the eve or during the period of the Burmese war there was no agreement or any sort of negotiation on the part of the British authority and the Princes of the royal family of Assam. Even Mr. Scott at his will proposed to the government of Bengal to restore the Ahom monarchy in Assam under the security and protection of the East India Company. The Burmese war taxed heavily and in that period the debt of the Company mounted up to nearly ten million pounds sterling. To solve the crisis Scott proposed for the retention of the lower parts of Assam which yield a revenue of more than three lakh rupees and Upper Assam might be annexed by the right of conquest and administered by the Barphukan of Gauhati almost independently. Finally in March 7, 1828 in an announcement Assam was annexed to the British dominion, and the question of surrendering Upper Assam to an Ahom prince was denied on the ground that, "since none of the aspirants did afford to the British any aid during the last war which could establish the slightest claim to a renunciation of any part of their right by conquest."[6]

It is evident that the British authority gradually succeeded to consolidate control over the whole region of Assam and the North-East. In the transformation of the internal social relations within the different communities, and the strategic and monopoly merchantile interests dragged Assam to a land of confusions and turmoil.

"About this time, to champion the cause of the nobility", narrates, the learned historian, Barpujari that, "there had emerged from an unexpected quarter the man of the hour Maniram Barua hitherto one of the most loyal official of the British Government. The energy, ability and intelligence of Maniram had attracted the attention of Captain Neufville who made him after the dismissal of Janardan Barbarua the Tahsildar and later Sherestadar at Jorhat. Maniran revealed his administrative genious in the revenue reforms which he immediately took up; he reorganized the confused 'khels', scrapped unnecessary expenses and tapped new sources of revenue. The receipt which could hitherto hardly meet the charges on the establishment gradually exhibited a surplus. In the war against the Khasis, the Bhutias and the Garos, Maniram rendered valuable services to the Government by supplying labours and provisions." This man of ability had to forego his job and refused to hold office under British and joined the Assam Tea Company at Nazira as the Dewan or chief executive. There he opened up several gardens and raised the profit and prestige of the company. Then he started a new venture by opening two tea gardens of his own at Jorhat but failed to obtain revenue concession like the previleged European planters. Deprived and frustrated Maniram then realized that under the foreign rule there was no future of his survival with a household consisting of 185 souls and his countrymen. With a vision to restore the former regime of the land he threw his fortune with the Maharaja Kameswar Singha, the son and the successor of Purandar Singha. "Leading all along a gay of life, the young prince is said to have squandered away the few pieces of silver and gold which his father had bequeathed to him, and is also reported to have quarreled with the widows of the family driving them to beseech the liberality of the British Government. Kameswar terminated his inglorious career in June 1851, leaving behind three widows and Kandarpeswar Singha alias the Charing Raja, a boy of eleven, burdened with a huge debt".[7]

In the middle of June, 1853, A.J. Moffat Mills, the judge of the Sadar Dewani Adalat, arrived Assam to look into the matters of the local administration. At that period Maniram submitted representations before the authority wherein, he in a loud voice actually expressed the lamentation and agony of the disgraced voiceless. Maniram states: "The upper and the middle classes have seen their offices abolished, their laguas and lixos taken away, male and female slaves set free...exemption and presumptive rights that had lasted for six hundred years removed, the fame and honour of respectable people destroyed and by making them pay revenue like other people they have been reduced to the greatest distress.

"It is supposed by giving pensions to some respectable Assamese great benefit has been conferred on them; but the fact is, that those who ought to have got pensions did not get any while those whose services had been of short duration and claims insignificant proved most successful".

In violent terms Dewan Maniram denounced the British government and bursted out:

"We are just now as it were in the belly of a tiger and if our misfortunes yielded any advantage to the Government, we should be content; but the fact is, there is neither gain to the people nor the government, and so long as the present state of things continue, we see no prospect of improvement in future."[8]

Maniram vehemently opposed the appointment of the foreigners like Mawaris and Bengalis from Sylhet as mouzadars, criticized the policy of introduction of taxes on opium and the destruction of the indigenous art, culture and religion. He also deplored the attitude of the government officials specially those in the military and stated that, "The bad temper of the young military officials is a source of much tribulations...their youth and indiscretion prevent their discriminating between good and evil or regarding with any consideration the manners and customs of the people."[9] He tried to convince the authority by every art of conviction that the restoration of the Ahom government in any form might be the only solution to save Assam from further degradation. For obvious reasons Moffat Mills took offence at the attitude of Maniram and suggested to the Government of India to inform the Charing Raja not to entertain any sort of hope for his restoration in future.

Mills' decision enraged Maniram against the British and

to plead the case of the Prince and of his own he left for Calcutta and arrived there in the early part of 1857. There he came in contact with the news of the flame and fire of the uprise of the Mutiny and took determination to free his motherland from the yoke of the foreign rule.

In the mean time the activities of the rebellious forces of Meerut, Kanpur and Delhi reached in the Brahmaputra Valley by different sources. The visitors, personal letters, newspapers even through the Fakirs the incidents of the mutiny in the form of harrowing tales spread over the region. As to the dissemination of the news, "I heard letters (were) read, they were in nagree... to this effect that all the country was taken by the king of Delhi and calling on them to do the likewise in Assam...the newspapers were read by the Sudder Ameen and the collector's Peshkar; and the Omlahs used to read them in the cutcherry and some of the sepoys used to go therein and hear. I used to read the Samachar Darpan...the Sahib (Mahony alias Masters) used to read to us the news in the Friend of India. Krishna Chandra Majumder, Vakeel, used to take...Peshkar's paper to his own house; near the man's is a house belonging to (a) Bramasari Fakir, where all the Fakirs of the place used to assemble. The Vakeel, above named, used to read the paper to them; all the Deswali sepoys, both Hindu and Mussulman, used to assemble there to talk over the affairs in India...."[10]

From the dispatches of the authority it is noticed that the sepoys of the Assam Light Infantry remained absolutely loyal and passive up to the month of August, 1857. In Assam the composition of the regiment was homogeneous. The majority of the sepoys were belonged to the different communities like Nepalee, Manipuree, Rabha, Jarrowa, Doaneah and other loyal tribes. The number of the Hindusthani sepoys in the Regiment were not so countable. The Commissioner of Assam was confident on the prevailing situation and in his report he stated in the month of June, 1857, that 'despite pressing invitation of the rebels, both the Regiments stationed at Gauhati and Dibrugarh had not only expressed their loyalty to the Government but even some of them also volunteered their services for joining in action against the rebels'. But when the news of the defection of Kunwar Singh of Jagdishpur and the outrage of the Danapur Regiment in Bihar arrived the sepoys, specially those who were from Arrah became restless. In the mean time Shaikh Bhikam, the Subedar of the detachment of Golaghat, in the district of Sibsagar, joined hands with Nirmal Hajari and Peali alias Mahesh Chandra Barua, the suspected agents of the prince Kandarpeswar Singha with a conviction to kill the Sahibs and to place the Raja as the King of the land. The message was hurriedly spread over the contingencies of Sibsagar, Dibrugarh and Saikhowa. The entire plot of the insurrection was planned guided by Maniram Dewan residing in Calcutta. Madhu Mallick, a Bengali Muktear, a close friend of Maniram was the prime architect behind the scene. The call was readily responded by Peoli Barua, Gandhi Barua, Kamala Barua, Nowbaisha Phukan, Saru Gohain, Ugrasen Gohain and many other dignitaries of different ranks and influence. Narrating the incidents Charles Holroyd reported to the authority: "In the month of Assar, Noor Mahomed Jamdr., of the Ist Assam Lt. Infy. came down from Deebrooghur to Joorhat on private leave and had interviews with the Raja regarding the assistance to be afforded to the sepoys, and of the remuneration they were to receive for placing him on the Guddee.

"In the month of Sawan (July-August), Roostam Singh Jamdr., and two sepoys went to Jorhat, and having visited the Saring Rajah by night, conferred with him regarding the arrangement made with Pealie at Golaghat. In the month of Bhadra, Debidutta Surmah Mouzadar (brother to Luckiedutta) received gold from the Rajah for the collection of Russud for the troops; for a similar purpose gold was also distributed to the other parties.

"In the month of Sawan Luckiedutta Surmah, brother to the Thakur of the Dewargaon Temple, received gold from the Rajah for performance of Poojah in the temple. The Poojah was actually performed, and about this time a list was made of the several temples and Shastes (Satras) to which Ghee and Oil was to be distributed for a similar purpose ... to accomplish which, money was paid by the order of the Saring Rajah."[11] Every attempt was also made to get the support of the Muslims who were supposed to possess number of muscats with them.

'In his deposition Maniran Sarmah, the Gandhia Barua, said that Bahadur Gaoburah received gold from Kandarpeswar to make a feast to the Mussalmans of Jorhat who were in possession of several guns. Danforth, the American Baptist, viewed the role of the Mussalmans: from a different angle. In his report to his Foreign Secretary, he wrote: 'Mussalman population are very impertinent, and tell the native Christians that the Co's reign is at an end, the Sahibs will be cut up, and Islamism once and forever established.'[12]

Barpujari described the situation as such, — "The preparations made by the rebels and the alarm thereof spread far and wide. The European planters, several of them, left their gardens and took shelter at Gauhati. The missionaries abandoned their churches; some of them made preparations to leave the country. 'We at Gauhati still alive', reported Danforth, the American Baptist, 'but we cannot say safe, the stroke may come at any moment.' The Commissioner of

Assam was rudely awakened about the middle of August 1857, on the receipt of a report from Holroyd to the effect that 'two or three native officers, commissioned and non-commissioned, of the first Assam Light Infantry on duty with a detachment at Golaghat, proceeding on leave through Joorhath, and on coming and going interview with the young Charing Rajah, Kandarpeswar Singha, and offered the assistance of the men of both the Regiments to reinstate him on his throne and maintain the country for him.' In a communique of 20 August, 1857, the Commandant of the Assam Light Infantry further reported: 'at this station (Dibrugarh) what I have all along expected has taken place an intended rise of the Muttocks and their intrigues also to get adherents."[13]

In this period of crisis there was not a single European soldier in whole of the North- East to protect the Englishmen. It was also a problem to sent troops from Calcutta for immediate help. Considering the alarming situation the authority urged upon the government of Bengal to despatch troops hurriedly to save the province from the threat of revolution. The authority in Calcutta forthwith sent on 11 September, European force of 104 men despatched to Dibrugarh under lieutenant Davis of whom half of the sepoys had some military training and the rest were seamen.

On the other hand the rebels finalised their plan of action to attack the targets in the early part of October when it was expected that Moniram Dewan would also reach Assam with arms and ammunitions. It was also planned, 'that Maniram was to be the Prime Minister... that Mudoo Mullick was to be immediately under him rank and position, that he (Peali) was to be the Barbhandar Barua, Lockeenath Hensoa Barua was to be the Nowbaisa Phukan, that Kamala Saringia Barua was to be made Subedar and Darogha of Jorhat... there would be no Khazna (revenue) but liksos as in olden times... no revenue on barilands and (only) one rupee per poorah on the rupit lands as in former times; that all the Sahibs from Gauhati upto Dibrugarh were to be (transferred) to Jorhat and made over to the Rajah. That Roostam Singh and Noor Muhammad were to be Subedars.... That Budram Subedar was to be made Subedar Bahadur.'[14]

On 29 August 1857 at about 9 p.m. the sepoys attacked the residence of Shaikh Bhikam. The incident as narrated by one native doctor, named as Keramat Ali who claimed himself as an eye witness, runs as follows, "On arriving, I saw a number of men collected in front of Subedar's house; in the midst the Subedar Shaikh Bheekun, Chunder Singh, the Jamadar of police, and Ramtohal Singh, the Kote Havildar, were seated in morahs; the rest being on the ground...Jelladar Misser, Bhola Panday and Sewsahai Singh (one after another) addressed the gathering...Hear brothers! If you are desirous of our own good and favour with the Rajah, you will listen to what we say and do what we tell you without drawing back; and whoever draws back or reveals anything shall be killed; and if he be a Mussalman, he will eat pig and if a Hindu he will eat cow, this shall be the curse on him...the others replied, what! Are we not born of man that we should desert the cause? ...let us sound the bugle and each man taking five Ghullali with him let us go this night to Jorhat; first cut Huronath Barooah's head off; it is said that Raghoobear Singh Jamadar is there with 20 sepoys and is loyal to the Government. We can make him join us, if not we will kill him; we will (then) go and put the Rajah on the throne...we will go at once to Sibsagar and first set fire to Holroyd sahib's house...and kill all the Europeans there; we will make the sepoys there join us and take the magazine and treasury. We can leave some men there to keep charge and go on with the rest to Debrooghur, there set fire to the houses and kill all the Europeans".[15] It is also learnt from the report of Danforth that, "The day was fixed to murder every European, and everything ready. In fact they were only waiting for the bugle to sound, to commence the work of death, when a slight circumstances occurred to lead them to decide on waiting for a few days for further information."[16]

But bugle was not sounded, confusions and chaos ultimately ruined the rebels. Immediately on receipt of the secret intelligence of the proceeding of the sepoys, the Commandant of the Assam Light Infantry arrested Shaikh Bhikan and other ring-leaders and removed them to Dibrugarh for the trial before a Court Martial. Raghubir Singh, who succeeded to the command of the detachment, was punished with vigorous measures of discipline.The authority ruthlessly dealt the matter and succeeded to establish their right of power and governance.

Meanwhile the Commissioner of Assam directed Holroyd to apprehend the Charing Raja; 'but the latter acted with circumspection lest any haste in the seizure of the Prince should precipitate a crisis. In early September 1857 Holroyd intercepted a bundle of letters written by Maniram Dewan or under his direction which authenticated the complicity of the Raja and the Dewan in a plot against the British. Accordingly on the midnight of September 7, with a party of 20 sepoys Holroyd took the boat and joined at Dikhowmukh a detachment under Captain Lowther and arrested Kandarpeswar and Madhumallick who resided in a rented house of Maniram Dewan at the nearby bazaar. The prince was conveyed on the same evening to Mahghur, wherefrom he was sent down to Calcutta and kept as a state prisoner at the Central Jail Alipur. This was followed by officials and non-officials in upper Assam–Peali Barua, the Marangikhowa Gohain, Mayaram Nazir, Dutiram Barua, Bahadur Gaoburah, Shaikh Farmud and several others–all alleged to have been participants, directly or indirectly, in the plot.'[17] When the arrest of the Raja was made known to the sepoys, the latter believed 'that he would be kept either (at) Dibrugarh, Tezpur, Seebsagar or Gauhati...wherever they took him, still he would be in their hands, for every where there are sepoys (Hindustanees)'.[18] They were also in false hope that Jung Bahadur, the Rana of Nepal, with a force 10,000 strong would be coming soon to their succor. Their hopes were doomed on the evening of 2 October 1857 when the Naval brigade arrived at Dibrugarh.

Again the outbreak of the 34th Native Infantry Regiment at Chittagong and the revolt of 73 Dacca regiment and their advancement towards the north made the authority alert in Assam and they were apprehensive of the repercussion which might have endangered the state of affairs in the neighbouring frontier tribes. The news of the Dacca fugitives and their march crossing the river Brahmaputra towards the South-West of Goalpara and the incidents that took place in and around Chilmari made the British fearful. The mutineers at Chilmari devasted the police station at Karaibari, plundered the bazaar and lifted the Jamadar and the sepoys attached to the outpost.

In the mean time the authority succeeded to take control over the entire situation. Whiting reported on 20 February, "The province is now quiet. About 200 sailors are in the valley; of whom sixty are at Jorhat, forty at Sibsagar and the remainder at Dibrugarh. Several sipahis have been transported for life. Several Assamese have also been transported for life; and Moniram, the chief instigator, who was at

Calcutta, has been brought up and being tried at Jorhat."[19] Dewan Maniram and Peali Barua were tried on 9 and 23 February and were sentenced to death. Both of them were hanged publicly on February 26. Madhu Mallik, Trinayan, Kamala Barua, Dutiram Barua, the Marangikhowa Gohain, Mayaram Nazir all of them were transported for life. Shaikh Formud Ali and Bahadur Gaobura, 'on charges of seducing the Mussalmans of Jorhat' were transported to Andaman and their properties were forfeited.[20]

The trial of Manirarm was a fierce. Holroyd the arch enemy of Dewan acted as both Prosecutor and Judge.The evidence on which he was convicted was insufficient and the accused was not given the chance of self defence. Dewan Maniram and Peali embraced the glorious death of Martyrs.Their patriotism and self sacrifice is contained in the folk memory. The bards, till today sing the stray songs in the hills and dales of Brahmaputra Valley and commemorate the sacrifice of their valiant heroes in folk- songs composed in Assamese.[21]

The King Gambhir Singh of Manipur was vested with the status of a sovereign ruler of his country on condition of the payment of Rs. 10,000 /- as tribute to the East India Company. He proved his loyalty and gratitude by rendering all possible help and service to the British at the time of the Burmese War. Considering the geo-political situation and the security of the Eastern Frontier part of the region, the British authority decided that, "The establishment of an independent government in Manipur in alliance with us would undoubtedly prove to be the most powerful and effectual check upon the Burmese government". David Scott, the Joint Magistrate of Rongpur was aware of the strategic and vulnerable position of the frontier pointed out, "the Assamese and the

Cacharees are, unfortunately, so timid and effeminate... that the defence of these countries must be provided for in great measure by extraneous means; the Nagas, the Singphos, the Khamtis and other tribes to the eastward of Assam are perhaps too little advanced in arts of civilization and of government to be able to make any effectual resistance against the numerous armies of the Burmese. Manipuries on the other hand are imbued with all Military spirit, that distinguishes the Rajput tribes of Northern Hindustan". Pemberton writes, "the history of Muneepoor, and the vicissitudes through which it has passed, the determined character of the people and their rooted aversion to the yoke of the Burmese are clearly shown.[22]

After the death of Gambhir Sing in 1834, his infant son Chandrakirti became the Raja of Manipur. Since then the throne became the center of conspiracy and turmoil. Senapati Nur Sing failed to succeed in the conspiracy was fled away from the country. In 1847 the British government warned the disgruntled Manipuri Princes in Cachar not to create disturbances in the district or on the border of Manipur, otherwise they would be transported to Bengal. Then Debendra Sing succeeded to the throne after the death of his brother Nur Sing.

In the mean time Chandrakirti Sing with his mother appeared in the scene with a determination to capture the throne by force. The British authority recognized the succession of Debendra Sing and decided to remove the mother and the former Raja from Manipur to Dacca.

Chandrakirti successfully escaped the arrest. And afterwards Captain MacCulloch, the Political Agent, withheld the recognition of Debendra Sing and Chandrakirti again succeeded to the throne of Manipur as de facto Raja. Frustrated

Debendra Sing and his brothers frequently made attempts to regain the lost power and threatened the supremacy of the authority. To overcome the situation MacCulloch made some propositions. He stated, "that in my opinion the establishment of good order and the maintenance of authority in this country can be effected only by the British government. In a country which, like this, owes its existence, and owns that it does so, to the British government, the influence of that government ought, I humbly conceive, to be paramount and capable of effecting this; but oft-repeated contests for the throne have lessened that influence, and will, I fear, if not prevented, destroy it eventually altogether: a successful attempt from Burma would do so at once.

"Towards the effecting of good order and maintenance of authority the stationing of British troops in Manipur would be the most effectual means. These troops however, could not be paid either in whole or part, and I have not contemplated this measure; but a more formal acknowledgment of the Rajah, with a declaration that he will not recognize as Rajah any Prince who by force may dispossess him, would, I think, prove a strong check upon these frequent attacks, would induce a feeling of security in the Authorities, and with that an inclination to improve rather than grind the people, and in this manner put a stop to these contests for the throne, so injurious to the country and British interests."[23]

At the period of Sepoy Mutiny 1857 the Rajah of Manipur was obviously loyal to the British. The authority was satisfied and recorded with note of appreciation that, 'the conduct of the Rajah during the mutiny was reported to have been praiseworthy, and the satisfaction of Government was accordingly expressed on this subject.'[24]

Tripura was an independent kingdom for long

centuries.The problems she had to face after the transfer of Bengal Dewani to the East India Company was primarily the border disputes with the adjoining district of Sylhet and Hill Tripura. In the year 1822, at the time of Lt. Fisher's survey, the king of Tripura strongly raised objection on the matter. The British authority laid down the principle for the arbitrators was that, 'all land included within the decennial settlement had been, and shall be, within the Company's territories'. Further, it was ordered, 'that the mere fact that any land had not been settled in 1790 should not alone be proof that it belonged to the Tripura state'. Mr Yule in his report submitted to the government in January 1851, proposed that, 'the country thus finally declared to be British territory, as consisting both of hill and plain covered for the most part with swamp and jungle. The hills however produced cotton, the cultivation of which might be greatly increased; while the plains bore here and there rich crops of rice not liable to inundiation; and also mustard and sugarcane.' Yule also strongly urged upon the government that, 'colonies of Manipuris or others should be encouraged to take it up on lease'.[25]

The State of Jayantia is situated in between Cachar and Sylhet. In 1774, Major Henniker attacked the independent state with a plea of some aggressions that took place against the inhabitants of the plains of Sylhet. In the year 1821, for the purpose of immolating certain British subjects from the Sylhet district, as per the version of the authority, some emissaries of the state were detected and punished. The Supreme government took this incident seriously and the Raja was cautioned and warned by the words that, 'any repetition of so horrible an offence would be followed by the immediate confiscation of his territory.'[26] When the Burmese invaded the territory of Cachar and intended to march to Assam through Jayantia, the British authority in Sylhet, came forward to a negotiation with the king. Mr. Scott, the agent of the Governor General, opened the talk with the condition that the Raja should follow the usual procrastinating policy of all natives before entering into the treaty and he was, 'promised the assistance of the government troops, if his own resources were actively employed in repulsing the enemy.' The Raja of Jayantia was also threatened with punishment if he allowed to enter the Burmese in his territory. It is interesting to observe that the British authority how nakedly came out with a false claim over the territory of Jayantia to manage the situation. Narrating the incidents Pemberton writes, "He (the Raja of Jayantia), had collected a force, which was said to consist of several thousands archers, but which most probably amounted to only a few hundreds; and he was conjectured to be favorable to the British power, though unwilling to compromise his independence by any engagements, until the destruction of his country, or compliance, became the only remaining alternatives.On the 2nd of February 1824, a letter was addressed by Mr. Scott to the Commander of the Burmese force in Cachar, prohibiting his entering in the territory of Jayantia, on the ground that the Rajah's ancestors had received that country as a gift after conquest from the Honourable Company; that he had himself sought British protection; and that the Burmese having openly threatened war, they could not be permitted to occupy that, or any other favourable position, for commencing hostilities."[27]

From his accounts it is also revealed that, the Burmese commander too sent a letter to the Raja claiming his presence in the Burmese camp, 'on the affirmed ground of his own known vassalage to the princes of Assam, which latter country had become tributary to Ava.' Shortly afterwards a party of Burmese troops appeared near Jayantia Frontier. In the mean time a detachment of 150 men, under a British officer was sent to the frontier to assist the Jayantia Raj and ultimately the Burmese force was withdrawn. Later in the month of April a treaty was signed with the Raja wherein he formally acknowledged his dependence and, 'pledged himself to abstain from all independent negotiations with any foreign power', and committed to provide with all sorts of help even with a military contingent in any war waged in the eastern part of the river Brahmaputra. Subsequently the Raja denied the treaty with the British and the authority took offence at this, and the disgusted Captain R. Boileau Pemberton in his report with anger states, "None of these conditions, however, did he fulfill with sincerity; and it was notorious that during the war he permitted a Burmese detachment from Assam to occupy his territory, in direct violation of the treaty which had preserved his country from the calamities that overwhelmed the less fortunate states of Kachar and Manipur."[28]

In 1830, at the confluence of the rivers Kopili and Dimla near Chaparmukh, Jayantia Raj established a Chowky and did not pay any attention to the repeated order issued by Mr. Scott and Robertson for its removal. Again in 1832, Chhatra Singha a dependent of the Raja of Jayantia, captured four subjects of the British and were carried to a temple of Goddess Kali for immolation. Among them three were sacrificed and one person was able to escape in Sylhet and reported the matter to the authority. Immediately the Government demanded the culprits and issued orders to Ram Singh, the Raja of Jaintia, which ended in a fruitless exercise. Then in November 1832 Raja Ram Singh died and his twenty years old nephew Rajendra Singh became the successor of the territory. The Britsh reminded him the acts of betrayal of his predecessor and finally decided to occupy the plains areas of Jayantia forcefully. "Firm however, in his determination not to surrender the guilty perpetrators of this most barbarous sacrifice, and led by a few crafty Bengalees to believe that they possessed influence sufficient to effect the restoration of his principality, he refused to continue in possession of any reduced portion of it"[29]. This attitude of Rajendra Singh made the authority furious and on the 15th of March 1835, Captain Lister, with two companies of the Sylhet Light Infantry, forcibly took possession of the independent territory and by a proclamation annexed the plains areas of the country to the British domination. By issuing an order on 30th March,1835, Jayantia was taken under the administration of the Political Agent, and Khasi Hills and Jaintia both the territories came under the Judicial control by the Khasi Hills Act VI of 1835. Raja Rajendra Singh was compelled to retire in Sylhet and the Company handed over to him his own personal property, amounting to more than one and half lac Rupees, as assessed by the authority. The people observed the incidents closely and became frustrated with the treatment of the British with their kings and expressed their love and affection to the Raja Ram Singh and Rajendra Singh in folk- songs and ballads. They portrayed the British as intruders and demons in their composition.[30]

During the period of Sepoy Mutiny 1857 when the news of the revolt of 34th Native Infantry Regiment and their advancement towards Sylhet and Manipur was received like other parts of North-East India the Khasi chiefs were also in belief that the British power in India is in danger and began to intrigue with some of them with the aim of recovering the lost territorial possessions. But the overall situation with the territory was remained peaceful. After the annexation of Assam Scott's negotiations with the Khasi chieftains made the territory an alley to the British. In fact the natural resources of the region allured the colonial administrators immediate after the annexation of Assam.The possibilities of improving and extending the agricultural and horticultural produce in the region elevated Mr. Scott and in 1830 he expressed his opinion as such: "These mountains are probably capable of producing opium at a cheaper rate, and of a better quality, than any part of our lowland possessions; the quantity obtained from a small patch of land, having been fully three times as much an equal extent of soil is capable of producing below. Wheat is also found to thrive well on the lower hills, and potatoes, turnips, and beet-roots, are produced in such abundance in the higher region, as to render the two latter most profitably applicable to feeding cattle during the winter months." Pemberton further added to more future prospects and mentioned that, "The mineral productions of this extensive region are too generally known, to require any particular mention here; they consist of inexhaustible supplies of the finest limestone procurable in India; of coal and iron, in scarcely less abundance; and slate and grey sandstone, particularly well adapted for building purposes. Years may elapse, are the full value of the controlling influence we have established in these hills becomes generally appreciated, or their resources fully developed; but we already begin to read the advantages of our position, in the cessation of those murderous visitations, which for years kept the border villages of Sylhet, and Assam, in a state of constant anxiety and alarm; and from which, we were liable to the erruptions of a horde of unknown barbarians, at moments when, struggling against the invasion of a formidable foe, from a more remote quarter, we might have been less able to guard our defenceless frontier and its timid inhabitants. The Cossyahs have now felt our strength; and having been severely punished for their treachery, have quietly submitted to the control it has been found expedient to exercise over them."[31]

The British first came in contact with the Garos among the hill tribes of Assam after the transfer of Bengal Dewani to the East India Company. After the occupation of Rangpur and Mymensing the British had to face fierce resistance from the people.

In 1775, one Mahammadan Fakir named Karim, declared himself as a reformer and sooth sayer. The Raja of Susung allowed him to live in Loterkandi where he got together a band of followers whom the neighbours called as 'Pagals' or Fools, and among themselves they addressed one another as Brethren (Bhai). In 1813 Karim was succeeded by his son Tipoo. Tipoo and his mother (called 'Mah Sahibah' or 'Lady mother' by the Pagals) both according to the local belief possessed miraculous power. Under their spells, wooden guns and swords turned into effective weapons in their hands and even the artillery fires had also no effect against them. The 'Lady mother' had only to blow on her clothes, and shake her under garment, to call a hidden army in to existence; and to her alone was restricted the power of seeing in to the future. It was perhaps from the want of this power, that Tipoo ceased to be a mere religious fanatic, and betook himself to more dangerous courses. 'He gradually formed a following of armed men, acquired much wealth by plunder, and perpetrated many crimes. In the state of the country, racked by the feuds of conflicting Zamindars, he formed a center of intrigue for all the discontented ryots. The Sherepore Zamindars had never carried out the permanent settlement rules, and always collected cesses from their tenants at their discretion. In November 1824, when called on by Government to provide supplies for troops passing to Assam to fight the Burmese, they made this as usual the excuse for imposing heavy extractions on the ryots. The ryots appealed to Tipoo who promised them a time when they should only pay nominal rents. On this the peasantry took up arms and entered in to closer alliance with the Paghuls, and began to refuse to give the customary tole of labour or pay rents'.[32] Among these ryots many of them were Garos who were settled on the low areas of Garo hills. In the month of January 1825 about 700 followers of Tipoo assembled at Sherpur and attacked the Zamindars of the locality. They raised arms against the abnormal enhancement of the rent. In the year 1793 the rent of these low land areas settled by the Gird Garos was fixed at Rs. 20/- and in 1825 it was paying Rs. 20,000/- to the Zamindars. In a fierce fight they heavily assaulted the Zamindars and then the district authorities intervened the situation to protect the mutual interests of both the Government and the Zamindars. After tough fights Tipoo was arrested and put into Jail and very soon he was also released. Then Tipoo raised a 'Royal Killah' made of bamboos, which is popularly known in Bengal as 'Banser Kellah', and raised his Jihad against the atrocities of the Zamindars and the British with his followers. The outrage of Tipoo was strongly dealt by the authority and was suppressed. Again in 1833 the followers of the 'Pagal-Panth' stirred up and caused to peasants insurrections.

Then again in 1836 independent Garos of Shibkujora launched a movement to stop the collections of tributes of the government and the Commissioner of Assam recommended for forceful submission of these turbulents. Narrating the actions taken by the government Alexander Mackenzie quoted from the Political proceedings, 25th July 1836, writes, "Scott's plan had (the Commissioner said) been to march into a village and give notice that if the chief did not surrender himself in two days and pay tribute, the village would be burnt and cultivation laid waste. In December he visited Singamari, where most of the Garo chiefs of that quarter came to meet him; and then enquiry proved that the most of the Garo disturbances had arisen from the oppressive conduct of our own native officers at the frontier markets."[33]

In the subsequent years of 1839, 1844 and upto the closing of 1856 the Garos of different groups raided in various occasion against the authority. Between the months of July and October 1852, they raided seven times in the frontier areas and killed fortyfour persons and made havoc of the life and properties. The British authority took offence of these incidents so seriously that Lord Dalhousie had to take review of the Garo policy in his hands. In fact the trade and revenue of the Company was affected for these disturbances and even 'the attempt to secure the upland Garos for the Frontier Police had also failed'. "The local authorities", writes Mackenzie, "proposed an expedition to demand the surrender of the principal offenders, to levy a fine on their village, or burn it in default of payment, to exact hostages and written engagements from the chiefs, and to survey the hills, and the education of Garos...An expedition was accordingly dispatched which burnt a village. As no overtures were made by the Garos for the surrender of the raiders, the Commossioner next proposed to government to the closing of the frontier markets. The objections to this plan in the case of the Garos was, that the no blockade however rigid could prevent them from getting supplies from Mymensing, while the innocent inhabitants of the plains, who depended for their livelihood on the cotton trade carried on with the Garos, were the principal sufferers".[34] Lord Dalhousie at that time recorded his opinion as such; "I have said that I deprecate these extreme measures, while anything else remained untried. But as these savages will neither treat, submit, nor rest, it is due to our own subjects, whose lives and property are in jeopardy, that we should have recourse to punishment, which though severe, is the only thing that they comprehend or feel. I consider that further military operations would be a waste of life uselessly. It is probable that the exclusion of the Garos from the plains will be effectual. It has been so when tried on the hill people on the opposite frontier of the North-West. I request, therefore, that they may be rigidly excluded from the plains, and that the Chiefs may be informed that the exclusion will be continued till satisfaction is made by the delivery of the murderers. They are at the same time to be informed that, if they are found in the plains while thus in resistance to the government, they will be seized and disposed of as the government may think fit. I am aware that these measures will probably inflict injury on the innocent while punishing the guilty. I regret it, but individual interests must yield to the public interests, when there is, as in this case, no alternative."[35]

The measures adopted by the authority was temporarily proved successful. Mackenzie rightly assessed the profit and loss business of his government; "It was found that the trade in cotton had become so material a source of profit to the Garos, that the closure of the haats was really felt as a severe punishment. They gave up some of the offenders and promised to arrest and deliver over the others."[36] Looking into the future prospect the government adopted adequate measure for 'the re-imposition of the old duty on cotton at the Garo markets.'[37]

But the hostilities of the people continued up to 1879. It is observed that between May 1857 and October 1859 nine numbers of assaults and raids were made and twenty heads taken by the Garos in the sorrounding localities. Narrating in brief about these incidents Mackenzie stated that, "however, they again recommenced, and were numerous and atrocious on both the Goalpara and Mymensing frontiers. On each occasion attempts more or less futile were made to procure the surrender of the offenders, but no comprehensive was laid down, nor was any vigorous effort made to change the nature of our relations with the hillmen."[38]

The simplicity of these hillmen, their folk-beliefs and their age old traditional weapons like spears, two-edged swords and the shields made of banana trunks were so helpless before the gun and the might of the British that Piannazi spared no words to ridicule them in his statement. He described the incidents that took place in a protected Garo village areas of Damukchiki where the independent Garos attacked a party of Surveyors in 1872. Piannazi narrates: "One of the last portions of the interior to submit was Rongreng. Rumour had reached those independent chiefs that Government soldiers had hollow spears that spat fire at a great distance; and Gwal, the bravest of them, who acted as a sort of commander-in-chief, was impressed by the news. He saw that a means of quenching those firing missiles must be found, and his fertile imagination was not long in hitting upon a good one. While chiefs and warriors were down-heartedly commenting upon the unwelcome news, he was busy heating up his spear and thrusting it, red hot, into a banana stem...sure enough the iron was cooling: hurrah!

Every Garo warrior was directed to bind large pieces of succulent banana trunks in two moist layers over his bamboo shield; and wild joy of the discovery swept fear away from the assembled tribesmen....It was very early morning. The sepoys had come up and were quietly camping in a clearing in the jungle some way from Rongreng village and the Garos planned to take them by surprise. In high spirits and full of confidence in their new shields, two-edged swords and spears in readiness, they stealthily crawled through the thick jungle and soon were near the camp.... A wild yell, a rush...but before they could reach the campclearing, the roar of a volley stopped them. Deafened and disconcreated by the noise, they halted and wavered. A second volley; groans near them; there on the ground prostrate on their banana shields lay Gwal and two of their bravest. Confidence melted away, fear of the mysterious fire-spitting spears again filled them, and shouting, scampering, throwing down their weapons they gave up their fight."[39]

The relation of the British with other minor hill tribes of North-East since 1826 up to the Mutiny period 1857 was also hostile. The policy of non-stop operation of, as Mackenzie advocated, 'iron fists in velvet gloves' as an order for 'succession of becoming' obviously invited confrontation. He also advised to take the policy of consolidation considering the fact that, "There was a pressing necessity of bringing under more stringent control the commercial relation of our subjects with the frontier tribes living on the borders of our jurisdiction."[40]

It is evident that the antagonistic attitude and the outrage of the people of the region was induced by the British policy of intervention and aggression in the territory of the land, economy, aristocrcacy and the culture. The hill people primarily depend for their livelihood on hunting, fishing, rubber-tapping, elephant catching and shifting cultivations etc. The colonial rule for their interest in trade and commerce occupied the vast land for tea plantation. It is observed that by the year 1871 more than three lakh acres of wasteland were settled with the tea planters on nominal fees or simple rates. On the other hand the land revenue on the ordinary farmers was heavily taxed. All these reports, incidents etc. etc. undoubtedly confirm the agenda of the land-hungry British Colonial Power and its mischevious governance in the garb of the policy of reformation and so called 'non-interference'. Obviously the people had to suffer terribly and the situations compelled them to act violently against the forceful imposition of the supremacy.

NOTES

1. Majumdar, Ramesh Chandra: *Sepoy Mutiny and the Revolt of 1857*, Calcutta, 1957, p. 88.
2. Gait, Edward: *A History of Assam*, Calcutta, 1926, pp. 327-28.
3. Chakravorty, Birendra Chandra: *British Relations with the Hill Tribes of Assam since 1858.*, quoted from Bengal Report for 1872- 73, Calcutta, 1981, p. 36.
4. Quoted from *Assam in the Days of The Company*, H.K.Barpujari, Gauhati, 1980, p. 204.
5. Barpujari, H.K.: *Assam in the Days of The Company*, Gauhati, 1980, p. 40.
6. *Ibid.*, p. 41.
7. *Ibid.*, pp. 174-75.
8. *Ibid.*, pp: 176-77.
9. *Ibid.*, p. 177.
10. *Ibid.*, p. 182-83.
11. *Bengal Judicial Proceedings*, July 29, 1858. No. 115; Holroyd to Young, June, 28.
12. Barpujari, H.K.: *Assam in the Days of The Company*, 1 Gauhati, 1980, p. 185.
13. *Ibid.*, p. 186.
14. *Ibid.*, p. 189.
15. *Ibid.*, p. 190.
16. *Ibid.*, p. 190.
17. *Ibid.*, p. 191.
18. *Ibid.*, p. 192.

19. *Ibid.*, p. 195.
20. *Ibid.*, p. 196.
21. See *appendix* A.
22. Pemberton, R.B.: *Report on the Eastern Frontier of British India. Second impression,* Gauhati, 1966, pp. 49-50.
23. Mackenzie, Alexander: *The North East Frontier of India*, New Delhi, 1999, p. 154.
24. *Ibid.*, p. 155.
25. *Ibid.*, p. 284.
26. Mackenzie, quoted from Pemberton, p. 217.
27. Pemberton, *Ibid.*, p. 220.
28. *Ibid.*, p. 221.
29. *Ibid.*, p. 222.
30. An excerpts of a popular song runs as follows:
    "Mui kai jaum re, kothaye gele tari
    Hakim haila hukumdar, peda praner bairi
    Batti-rutti Indra Singh re, mukhe rekha dari
    Bandi kari thaila niya, Murari Chander bari
    Mui kai jaum re" —

    —Where I will go for shelter and protection. Hakim (the British) is now the all powerful administrator. Our beloved king Indra (Rajendra) Singh, the young, short and stout, whose beards are not yet prominent on his face, has been arrested and kept confined in the house of Murarichand (Dewan). Oh, where I will go—

    [Quoted from, Kar, Subir, *Uttar Purba Bharater Loka Sahitye Bidroha Chetana.* "Loka Charyya", p. 26, Guwahati, 2003.]
31. Pemberton, *Ibid.*, p. 264.
32. Mackanzie, Alexander: *Ibid.*, p. 255.
33. *Ibid.*, p. 255.
34. *Ibid.*, p. 257.
35. *Ibid.*, p. 257.
36. *Ibid.*, p. 258.
37. *Ibid.*, p. 259.
38. *Ibid.*, p. 259.
39. Chakravorty, Birendra Chandra: *op. cit.*, p. 34.
40. Mackanzie, Alexander, *op. cit.*, p. 56.

2

Mutiny Period in Sylhet-Cachar: An Historical Approach

In the Mutiny period 1857-1858 though the British authority in the district of Sylhet and Cachar was apprehensive and the hostility and commotions were very much prevailed in the region yet finally no one took arms against the Raj. But it is evident that the common people and a few feudal Zamindars were very much sympathetic towards the uprise of the sepoys and offered shelter and food to the fugitives who revolted at Chittagong. Again, there were loyal Zamindars like Syeed Bukht Mujmadar, Choudhury of Sylhet, Zamindar of Maina of Pratapgarh Pargana who rendered all possible services to the British; Suruz Mian of Biskut and Kalamia of Latu, who proved to be traitors and like many others in the valley who harvested their fortune in those days of the Mutiny. Among the elite families of the district of Sylhet, the "First and foremost of the high families of this country stands the Mujmadar family," narrates, Babu Shambhu Chundur Dey, "Even when the British flag was hoisted in the land, the family seems to have received due honour at the hands of the foreign conquerors. Some of its members had been appointed to high posts which they appear to have enjoyed for a pretty considerable period. In the present day, too, the family is held in due esteem. Moulavee

Hameed Bukht Mujmadar was a faithful and zealous servant of Government and said to have been to Sylhet what Sir Abdul Ghani is to Dacca."[1]

The kingdom of Cachar came under British rule in 1832 and the territory was treated as unsettled area. The land revenue system of this district was quite separate from Bengal Zamindary system and landed aristocracy like other parts of the country was not developed. For obvious reasons other than the disgruntled Manipuri princes we do not find any role of the vested interested feudals in the mutiny period in this region.

The learned historian Rajani Kanta Gupta in his account narrated the revolt of the 34th Native Infantry Regiment, at Chittagong as such, "At Chittagong the 34th N.I. Regiment revolted suddenly on 18th November. The Commissioner of the regiment failed to dissuade them from taking part in anti-government activities. Listening the news of the outbreak, the Captain of the Regiment and the other British officials betook themselves in the adjacent forest range. The mutineers plundered the treasury, released the convicts of the Jail, burnt down the Barrack, looted the armoury and then flew towards Tripura. Habildar Rajabuli Khan led the rebels. No British people was killed or harassed except one Barakandaz who was murdered while attempted to prevent them from arson. Meanwhile, the Commissioner of Chittagong sent messages to the authority at Calcutta for reinforcement. He also sent letters to the neighbouring independent king of Tripura and other two headmen of the tribal areas to resist the mutineers. In the meantime the fugitives arrived at Sitakunda and turned their directions towards the North-East and took refuge in the hills of Tripura. They believed that within the independent territory their lives would be more safe and protected. But this belief was far from real state of affairs, and any sort of harassment was beyond their knowledge and apprehension. The maharaja of Tripura did not waist time to show his allegiance to the British and sent a large number of troops to resist the rebels. Being defeated they fled through the hill range of Comilla and advanced towards the north. On the way suffered terribly. Many of the convicted prisoners of the Chittagong Jail, who were with the rebellious troops, were arrested. Three elephants and a sum of about ten thousand rupees were captured. The dejected mutineers then rushed towards the independent kingdom of Manipur. On the way they plundered one police station. The Government had a serious look on the movement and having received the news of the advancement of the rebel force, Mr. Allen, the then Commissioner of Sylhet district, forthwith sent his infantry to attack them. On December 15, Major Byng led the army and rushed towards Pratapgarh, eighty miles away from the Sylhet Sadar Station. After his arrival the Major learnt from a reliable source that the mutineers flew towards Latu Police Station, twenty miles northeast of Pratapgarh. At once he marched back with his force and arrived at Latu. There a fierce fighting took place between the two forces. The anguished mutineers tried to win over the native soldiers of the Sylhet Light Infantry, by *appealing to their religious sentiments and nationality,* but the answers they received was only bullets. In that severe encounter Major Byng lost his life and the mutineers met with heavy casualties. Many of them were killed and arrested. The remaining ones flew towards Manipur. A group of the Infantry followed the rebels and the rest turned back to the Sadar Station at Sylhet. The 54th British Army Battalion which was sent from Dacca and Chittagong for reinforcement were called back subsequently.

On January 9, 1858, the Sylhet Light Infantry attacked the fugitives at the border of Cachar and Manipur. The fighting took place for two hours. Being defeated, they again flew towards the adjacent hill range. Eight days later, another encounter took place and that was the last blow. Zamadar Jogbir Singh led the British troops and finally succeeded to uproot the mutineers of the 34th Native Infantry Regiment of Chittagong."[2]

Narrating the incidents E.A. Gait informed that, "The rebels, numbering about two hundred, came up soon afterwards. *They tried by taunts and solicitations to prevent the Hindustanis, who formed half the detachment, but only answer they received was steady fire,* which put them to flight with a loss of twenty six killed. Major Byng was also killed."[3]

Achyut Charan Choudhury Tatwanidhi narrates the intrusion of the mutineers in the district of Sylhet and Cachar and the incidents that took place in these areas in details in his book *'Srihatter Itibritta'*. He writes in Bengali, that at Chittagong three hundred soldiers revolted being persuaded by the Mutiny of the western provinces. They looted a sum of Rs. 27,8267.00 from the treasury of Chittagong and had released the prisoners from the Jail and then flew through Tripura and entered in the district of Sylhet. At Langla, in Sylhet district, these rebels collected 'rasad' from the zaminder Gauch Ali Khan, the father of Maulavi Ali Ahmed Khan. This incident aroused suspicion in the minds of the authority about their involvement in the rebellion. Subsequently, at great pains and sufferings, the zaminder family had to submit to the Government. Major Byng of Sylhet Light Infantry marched towards Pratapgarh Pargana with his force to coerce the mutineers. When the infantry arrived at Pratapgarh, the soldiers were busy in preparing their meals.

All on a sudden, acting on a secret information, the Major ordered for immediate march for Latu. Leaving behind the half-cooked meal the Infantry went into action. The report that the rebels had been approaching at Latu was transpired to the authority by the Choudhury family of the village Maina of Pratapgarh. Narrating the source of information, the writer notes that the news about the whereabouts of the rebels were communicated by one Kalamia, a muslim ryot of his ancestor. The British soldiers met the rebels near Latu bazar. Immediately the mutineers took shelter on the top of the hillock Malegarh and opened fire on the infantry. The British soldiers were in a disadvantageous position. They stationed themselves on the bank of the river below the hill. On the first attack Major Byng and five other soldiers of the Sylhet Light Infantry lost their lives and one more was seriously injured. At last the gallantry of the subedar Ayudhya Singh succeeded to overcome the enemy. The mutineers then took their flight towards Cachar. In this encounter twenty six lives of the rebel force were lost.[4]

Ratanlal Chakrabarty of Bangladesh, stated in his account the incidents of Chittagong mutiny, 1857, and its follow-up and reactions in the district of Sylhet. From his account it is learnt that the mutineers were offerded shelter and food by the virtuous Zamindar Gouch Ali Khan of Langla (Maulaviganj) in the District of Sylhet. On this charge Ali was arrested and but for insufficient evidences later on Allen was compelled to release him.[5] The arrest of Gouch Ali created serious resentment among the influential Muslims of the District and they were determined to release him applying force. From the proceedings of one of the arrested sepoy of the rebel force, it is also revealed that a plot of conspiracy against the British was planned secretly and Zamindar Gouch Ali was ready to join the mutineers with his five thousands retainers.[6] The news of the arrival of the mutineers alarmed the British men of Sylhet. One Sayed Bakt Mazumdar of the town, and his eldest son Hamid Mazumdar brought out their six numbers of cannons to met the challenges. But the district authority noticed these activities of the Mazumdar family suspiciously and seized these cannons from their possession.[7]

From all the dispatches of Captain Stewart, the then Superintendant of Cachar, informed us in details the activities of the Mutineers of 1857 and the British forces in and around the district. In a letter addressed to the Governor General Bengal, Stewart stated that, "the popular mind in Cachar seems in no way affected by the disturbances which are occurring in the North-West. The Bengalee proclamation received by me was duly distributed, and the condition of the district is as peaceable as it possibly could be, there being no appearance of popular movement or excitement deserving of any notice."[8] Immediately after receiving the report of the revolt of the three companies of sepoys at Chittagong and their advancement towards the North-East, the district authority became apprehensive of the situation. Stewart then on December 7, 1857, posted guards at the Southern part of the border and sent a small party to the Lushai villages with the message that, "If men come to them through the jungle from the West with red coats and heavily laden, they are our enemies and must be opposed in every possible way, if it is the wish of the Lhoochais to endeavour to please our Government. That the men themselves are most probably wealthy, and it will afford easy and good plunder, and that moreover I will give Rs. 50/- for each sepoy for whom they account to me."[9] In the earlier dispatches though the authority expressed that, "all remain quiet in Cachar" yet they were anxious with the secret activities of the Manipuri princes who took their refuge in the district. Stewart, therefore, urged upon the Authority in Bengal for posting of more troops in the district. Narrating the complicacy of the situation he wrote, "Rumour says that an invasion of Manipoor has been projected among the Manipoories of Cachar, and that it is intended that an attack should in the first place be made on the Magazine here for the purpose of obtaining a supply of ammunition for the expedition."[10]

On December 19, Stewart had received a letter from Mr. Dodd that, "the 34th Native Infantry, informing me that, after having marched to Pertabghur. Major Byng's force upon certain information received countermarched to Latoo on the river Kasiara, and there had an engagement with the mutineers on the morning of the 18th, in which they were completely routed with a losse of about 30 men. The remainder had fled, it was said in the direction of Pertabghur with a view to make towards Cachar and Munipoor."[11] He also informed that he had received a letter from the Daroga of Latu wherein it was intimated that, 'the mutineers had passed the night of 19th December at Deuliabond,' Sylhet, "apprising me of their (mutineers) having gone eastward with a view to cross over the hills into my pergunnah of Serespore and Hyliakandi."[12] On December 21, 1857, Lt. Ross informed Stewart that the mutineers were split into three to four different groups and all were trying to enter into the district of Cachar. One of three groups comprising of forty to fifty strong soldiers were approaching towards Badarpur. Stewart then reinforced his strength at Panchgram. On 21st evening, having heard of the news that the Mutineers were in the village Chandpur in Sarespur Pargana and were trying to march towards Hailakandi, Lt. Ross rushed with fifty numbers of strong arm and twenty five Kuki scouts. The troops arrived at Companyganj on 22nd morning. In the meantime the mutineers had crossed the Valley during the night. He then marched towards Mohanpur Mouza and intercepted the rebels. In the encounters on official side one sepoy was killed, three sepoys were injured and one was missing. Some dozen of the mutineers faced heavy casualties and the remainder escaped in the dense forest to the south-east direction.[13] On the hill-top where the fight was taken place between the mutineers and the British force is popularly known as **'Rantila'**, situated on the river side of Dhaleswari.

Consequently on Lieutenant Ross' departure the Sadar Station Silcher being weakend, Stewart made arrangements to strengthen the Head Quarter had withdrawn several guards from the North East and the outpost of Jalenga was replaced by 12 armed Kukis recruited from the villages in the grant of The Cachar Tea Company. It may be mentioned here that The Cachar Tea Company had received a grant of 12,508 acres on 1st May, 1856 from the Government. During the period of Mutiny they were conducting their survey works. As a recognition of their loyal service the Company received a further land grant of 160508 acres.[14]

On December 24, the fugitives arrived at ***Jalenga valley***. The helpless mutineers were, at that time, unable to drag themselves in the miserable situations. At afternoon the government force again attacked them and killed numbers of the rebel sepoys. Being defeated the fugitives took their flight towards the great lake of **Chatla** leaving behind few muskets, a few bags full of money and huge number of baskets full of rice.[15]

Appreciating the excellent performances of Sylhet Light Infantry throughout the engagements which took place, Stewart remarked, "Distant not more than 30 yards from the enemy while firing, the latter tried to gain them over by every art of appealing to their ***religious feeling*** as well as ***nationality.*** Failing this they taunted them by calling them *"KRISTIAN KA KOOTAS"* and *"GOLAMIES"* but they received answer only in bullets and abuse."[16]

In fact, Stewart was worried about the reinforcement of sepoys and expressed his opinion in the report wherein he stated that, "The mutineers are still 200 hundred strong with abundance of arms and ammunition and I have not anything like equal numbers to oppose them. Superior numbers are required in order to surround them in the jungle, else it will be nothing but a running fight the whole way through to Munipoor, whither it is now certain that the 34th are bent upon going under the mistaken impression that they can go to Munnipoor to Nepal and hence to their own country. I am not even strong enough to dispatch a force after them should they get out of my district and pursuing force would be most desirable."[17] It is also learnt from the official version that the people of the district were much alarmed, particularly the Bengalees were in great fear, Stewart remarked on the situation and commented that "The budmashes are all on the look out for a favourable opportunity to plunder and one considerable dacoity has already taken place." [18] But the Manipuries of Cachar were anxious to take hold of this opportunity to carry out their plans to invade Manipur. In the dense jungle of Chatla Haor the fugitives were wandering helplessly for about five days. They were tracked up by Kuki Scouts and reported that during that period the rebels, "did not obtain one particle of nutritious food, but were compelled to eat jungle roots and berries."[19] The Scouts also came across several of rebels who had died of hunger and disease and also on the bodies of many of their children whom the fugitives on their flight had dashed on the ground being unable to carry on. They also arrested one ***kaider*** and a *Seikh Faqueer* of Chittagong.[20]

It may be recalled in this connection, the unfortunate tragic situation of the fighters who dedicated themselves for the liberation of the country from the foreign rule is echoed in the melancholy voice of the village bard in the words, 'Jaingaya kandere banar ghash khaiya'–Oh! The warriors are crying and passing all through the ways taking the jungle roots and berries to meet their appetite.

The mutineers then took their refuge in the jungles of Pargana Banraj. Captain Stevens was posted there in the surroundings with one hundred sepoys at Sonai Mukh. He was instructed to proceed to their rear and drive them down upon where at the village Nagdin Gram Lt. Ross was already placed himself with whole force. On December 31, while Captain Stevens and Lt. Ross attacked the mutineers the latter immediately took their flight and crossed the river Sonai and enter in the deep forest on the Eastern side of the hills of Bhuban- range. In the meantime a Jamadar of Sylhet Light Infantry with 16 numbers of sepoys were dispatched from Sylhet. On the way to Silchar they met 10 numbers of rebel sepoys who had separated from the main group after Latu massacre were charged at Mohanpur in Hailakandi and killed 8 of them and other 2 were arrested.[21]

On the other hand, in his dispatch, on the basis of the report received from Major McCulloch, Stewart informed the authority that, the Rajah of Manipur, "has dispatched 400 men towards his frontier to give assistance and to cut off the mutineers should they cross the border. His force has been placed under my orders and I have directed the Major Commanding to confine his operations solely in the Munnipoor territory. He has my orders to halt at Noonshinbong, and to send to Luckipoor for provisions, where I have made arrangements to supply him, and also 100 men of Sylhet Light Infantry, should it be necessary to send them in to Munnipoor after the rebels".[22]

It is also learnt from the reports that 3 or 4 numbers of Bengali were associated with the mutineers for the purpose of showing the way towards Manipur. Captain Stewart then directed the Major Commanding of the Manipur force to depute 100 sepoys on the confluence of the river Jeeri and Barak. On January 12, 1858, the mutineers with Narindrajit Singh the prince of Manipur, and his followers came out from the jungles and entered into a village to the west of Binnakandi at morning. Immediately after their flight a heavy engagement took place.

Narrating the incidents Captain Stewart wrote that, "This party while proceeding along the northern bank of the river, a short distance from Luckipoor, was fired upon by the mutineers from the opposite bank. This fire was returned by Lt. Binst and the enemy engaged in front. Lt. Ross then advanced from Binnacandy along the southern bank of the river, and attacked their right flank. Captain Stevens and Lt. Binst crossing the river in rafts under cover of this attack, and an action took place which lasted for two hours. The mutineers were beaten from house to house in the village they occupied and at last dispersed and fled back in to the jungles to the south, pursued by our troops as long as it was practicable."[23]

After gaining over the situation Stewart had appreciated the Kuki Levies along with the Sepoys of the Sylhet Light Infantry for their performances. He also expressed loudly his extreme satisfaction with Captain Stevens for his undaunted spirit and commenting on the achievement he wrote to the authority in Calcutta, "I am sure his Honor will perceive that, to the European officers leading the force, the greatest credit is due for the promptness and precision with which they acted, and which secured a victory so decisive and effectual."[24] He had also recommended for approval and recognition of the gallant services and loyal conduct of the troops and the Officers who led them.

From his dispatch a very striking information is revealed which acknowledge the dubious role of the Engrej who boasted for their service towards humanity. In his letter appreciating the service of one doctor Stewart with a special note wrote, "Doctor Shircore was present with the force in the double capacity of medical officer and in charge of the intelligence department. To his indefatigable exertions Captain Stevens is indebted for the good information which he has all along received of the position and design of the enemy."[25]

Though victory was gained over the helpless mutineers, the situation in the district was not free from troubles. Particularly the Manipuri Princes were secretly organizing their strength to invade Manipur. In his statement Stewart reported that the mutineers who were apprehended from the different parts of the district were tried, sentenced and executed by himself upto 13th of January 1858 under the provision of Act XVII of 1857. This Act being experienced as improper and insufficient to cope with the situation, he requested the authority to strengthen his powers by supplementing the Act XI of 1837. He came forward with a prayer on January 16, 1858, wherein he stated that, "as it is now apparent that the portion of our own subjects in this district are in rebellion against the Government, I have the honor to solicit that you will suggest to the Lieut. Governor the expediency of investing me with powers under ACT XI of 1837 for the trial of such as may be apprehended."[26]

The interim report submitted by Stewart, dated February 13, 1858, reveal the attitude and the nature of the trial from which a correct assessment of the proceedings can be made. Stewart wrote that, "I have engaged in scouring the jungles in this vicinity with Scouts and mounted sepoys and have succeeded in accounting for the 6 mutineers, making a total of 185 killed since entering Cachar, in the following manners:

a.	Tried and executed by the Civil authority	:	14
b.	Killed in action	:	57
c.	Found dead in the jungles	:	08
d.	Killed by Scouts in the field	:	37
e.	Brought in by troops, both Govt. and Munnipoories, Scouts, Kookies and villagers, and shot by sentence of Drum Head Court Martial	:	69
		Total:	185

2. The list of camp followers taken stands now as follows:-

Regimental Bheestie	1	Transportation for 14 years
,, Barber	1	,, ,, life
,, Bunnia	1	,, ,, 7 years
Sepoy's son	1	,, ,, ,,
Sheikh Faqeer	1	Awaiting Trial
Cittagong convicts	10	,, ,,
Women	13	,, ,,
Children	11	(two since dead)
Total:	39"[27]	

It is also learnt from the report that about 110 and 120 stands of arms were also seized from the enemy and about Rs. 30,000.00 of the plundered Chittagong treasure were recovered by the authority. Since the mutineers entered in

Cachar, 185 of them were killed and 44 lost their lives in encounters in the district of Sylhet and Tripura.[28]

On January, 24, 1858, the British force killed many rebels and arrested two of them in an encounter at Jalenga Valley. These two were tried and sentenced to death after two days' retention. Stewart himself conducted the court and the convicts were shot dead in his presence.

At Tillain, now known as Masimpur or Arunachal, in the district of Cachar, in an encounter lasting for three days many fugitives were killed and captured. The wounded and arrested persons were tried on the same day shooted down in presence of the villagers who were summoned to witness the consequences. This way the British authority tried to refrain the common people from showing sympathy to the mutineers. In order to terrorise them they usually hanged or shot to death the rebels in an open or public place before a gathering of mass whom they summoned to witness the severity of the punishment. Jyotirmoy Sen gives us details of such brutal act of the authority and narrates. "In order to create horror and terror in the heart of the commonman the fourteen mutineers who were executed after the trial by the Civil authorities of Cachar were hanged on the branches of the big pippal tree, stood on the north–west corner of the present Sadar Police Station of Silchar. A huge congregation of villagers were made together round the spot by the beat of drums to witness the consequences of the rebellion against the British Raj. In the same manner two sepoys were hanged on the branches of a pipple tree at a place on the bank of the river Dhaleswari at Companyganj."[29]

From the above statements of the history and the historical records we can summarize the fact that in November 18,

1857, the 34 Native Regiment stationed at Chittagong, mutinied against the British Raj and being defeated plundered the treasury, looted the armoury, broke open the Jail, arrived in Sylhet through Tripura and Comilla. At Latu a fierce fighting took place with Sylhet Light Infantry led by the Major Byng. In this encounter Major Byng and many of his sepoys were killed. The mutineers also met heavy casualties. Many of them were killed and arrested. Ultimately they had to flee towards the district of Cachar with the intention to join the disgruntled Manipuri princes Narindrajit Singh and other adjoining tribal chiefs who were engaged in the confrontation with the British at that time.

The Zamindars of the district Sylhet, like Gouchali Khan of Langla, Choudhury family of Gulam Rabbani of Badarpur were sympathetic towards the rebellious force and they offered them food and shelter while the most notable Mazumdar family was engaged in loyal services; and the Choudhuri families of Pratapgarh, the Zamindar Kalamia and the Doctor Shircore acted as informers of the British. All these incidents casted a deep impact on the people of the region and they expressed their actions and reactions in various means particularly in the traditional form of folk-songs and ballads.

NOTES

1. Dey, Sambhu Chundur: *Majmudar Family of Sylhet*, pp. 13-14 Printed and Published by, K.C. Roy, New Pardarshak Press, Sylhet, 1894.
2. Gupta, Rajani Kanta: *Sipahi Juddher Itihas*, Vol. IV., pp. 209-11, Calcutta, 1910.
3. Gait, Edward: *A History of Assam*, Calcutta,1926, p. 328.
4. Choudhury, Achyutcharan: *Srihatter Itibritta*, Vol. II, Chapt. III, Calcutta, 1917, pp. 50-51.

5. Chakraborty, Ratan Lal: *Sipahijuddha O Bangladesh*, Dhaka, 1984, p. 85. Quoted from the letter addressed to the Commissioner of Chandannagar Circuit by the Magistrate of Sylhet, letter dated 15th December, 1857; Bangladesh Secretariate Records, Sylhet District (Judicial Proceedings), Vol. 3, pp.138-49.
6. *The Dacca News*, June 19, 1858, p. 302.
7. Ali, Sayeed Murtaza: *Hazrat Sahjalal O Sylheter Itihas*. Dacca, 1965, p. 133.
8. Choudhury, Sujit, (ed.): *The Mutiny Period in Cachar*, Silchar, 1981, p. 72, Despatches of Capt. Stewart, the Superintendent of Cachar, dated, June 10, 1857.
9. *Ibid.*, Despatches, dated, Dec. 7, 1857, p. 4.
10. *Ibid.*, Despatches, dated, Dec. 7, 1857, p. 5.
11. *Ibid.*, A letter to the Secretary to the Government of Bengal, Fort William, Calcutta, dated, Dec. 22, 1857, p. 6.
12. *Ibid.*, Despatches of R. Stewart, dated, Dec. 22, 1857, p. 7.
13. *Ibid.*, Despatches, dated, Dec. 1857, p. 9.
14. *Ibid.*, Despatches, dated, Jan. 16, 1858, p. 23.
15. *Ibid.*, Despatches, dated, Dec. 22, 1857, p. 8.
16. *Ibid.*, Despatches, dated, Dec. 22, 1857, p. 10.
17. *Ibid.*, Despatches, dated, Dec. 24, 1857, pp. 11, 13.
18. *Ibid.*, Despatches, dated, Dec. 26, 1857, p. 12.
19. *Ibid.*, Despatches, dated, Dec. 24, 1857, p. 13.
20. *Ibid.*, Despatches, dated, Dec. 26, 1857, p. 14.

    [In the margin of the letter names of eight other arrested sepoys were mentioned. They were Sroop Sing, Ramdeen Sing, Pariak Sing, Dameer Sing, Rajcoomer Sing, Sorra Ram, Kujunrer Sing and Luchmen Sing.]
21. *Ibid.*, Despatches, dated, Jan. 2, 1858, p. 17.
22. *Ibid.*, Despatches, dated, Jan. 2, 1858, p. 18.
23. *Ibid.*, Despatches, dated, Jan. 13, 1858, para-3, 4, p. 20.
24. *Ibid.*, Despatches, dated, Jan. 13, 1858, para-13. p. 22.
25. *Ibid.*, Despatches, dated, Jan. 13, 1858, para-7, p. 21.
26. *Ibid.*, Despatches, dated, Jan. 16, 1858, para-10, p. 24.
27. *Ibid.*, Despatches, dated, Feb. 13, 1858, p. 35.

28. *Ibid.*, Despatches of Stewart to Capt. Dewaul, Commanding, Detachment, Late 34th N.I., Chittagong, dated, Feb. 17, 1858, p. 37.

29. Sen, Jyotirmoy: *Untold Story of Mutineers in Cachar*, Raijor Batori, Published by the Directorate of Information and Public Relations, Gauhati, Nov. 18, 1975, p. 49.

3

Folk-Tradition and the Ballad: Its Source and Origin

Linguistically and culturally Surma-Barak valley is a part of Bengal. The valley is resourceful for its unique folk-literary traditions. There are evidences that the whole Region is known throughout Bengal as well as the North-East Region of the country for its traditional folk-songs, ballads, tales, folk-arts etc. The doctrine of Sri Chaitanya and Sufism influenced the region remarkably. Nabadwip, the seat of Hindu religion and culture in Bengal was resorted to freely by Brahmin youths of Sylhet. Sukreswar and Baneswar the two learned brothers of the village Dhakadakshin were appointed as the court poets by the king of Tripura to compile the history of Tripura Royal family. Pundarikaksha Sarma alias Adwaita Acharjya, the son of the courtier of the king Divya Singha of Laur, went over to Nabadwip and started a social and religious movement of re-organisation and reformation. The teaching of Sri Chaitanya guided the entire literary and cultural thoughts of the people of the region for centuries. Both Hindus and the Muslim bards composed innumerable songs being inspired and influenced by the love episode of Radha-Krishna and portrayed them as an idol of eternal love. Besides, they composed lyrics on mythological plots, ballads on local historical events, natural atrocities and various other songs on the everydays' phenomenon of life. *Dhamail, Bau-nach (Bride-Dance) Choupara kirtan, Nrityas of Gopal - Gobinda Bhog etc.* are treated as the most oldest folk-songs and dances of the valley. *Jari, Sari, Baramasi, Matrimonial-rituals, Mystical religious, Jhumur, Manasar-Geet,Ojha-danc*e and various types of love songs are the traditional folk-culture of the Valley. *Murshida* and *Marifati* are also the most popular songs of a variety of *Sufism,*was developed in the region since the period of Darbesh Shahjalal and his follower 360 Aulias. These songs which are allied to the Hindu Vedantism, found more favour with the Bengali Mussalmans, who are mainly converted to Islam from Hinduism. Among the most popular composer and bards of these type of songs are Hasan Raja, Sitalong Shah Arkum Shah, Fakir Irfan Ali, Akil Shah, Fakir Nilam Shah, Syed Shah, Bhela Shah, Madan Shah are most noteworthy. Among the Hindus, Baul Radha Raman, Sadananda, Suhag Das, Dina Bhabananda,Durga Charan Das, Chaitanya, Bipin, Baneswar,Vaishnab Das are famous as composer and singer of the folk-poetry of the region. Besides, there are other types of traditional folk-songs popularly known as *'Bhatta-Kavya'* or *Bhat-gan* and *Lacharigan*. The poets and Bhattakabis are called *'Bhats'*. They, actually, like the Charanas of Rajputana, kept up the memory of shining historical events in metrical ballads at a time when printing technology was unknown. Sylhet was the recognized seat of those *Bhats* in Bengal, and no place in the district was as famous for this type of ballads as Baniyachang, and no Bhat achieved there higher laurel than Makaranda, the Prince of the ballad composer of the age gone by. There are villages named as Bhatpara, Bhateswar, Bhatgram etc. in the valley, which reminds the glorious tradition of the past. Bhatsongs like *'Rajnagardhanser kabita'* and *'Nirannabbui Saner Girair Kabita'* are popular among these types of ballads. The Bhats were mainly Brahmin by caste, but there were Muslim Bhats too. *Rajnagar Dhanser Kabita'* was composed by Bhatta Joychandra based on a historical incident and Bhat Kabi Arkum Ullah composed *'Nirannabbui Saner Girair Kabita'* on the event of the famine of 1299 B.S. The most notable *'Lacharigans'* are also ballad in form and character. These are also composed on the facts based on the historical incidents. Among these the most popular ballads are – *'Katumiyar gan', 'Pulak Jaluar gan', 'Binanda Rajargan', 'Kamal Ranir gan', 'Hirachand Sadagar', 'Dewan Adam Khan', 'Manai Haria', 'Amir Asfar', 'Dhanai Sadhu', 'Narsingha Raja', 'Dulvi Kanya', 'Himaliya Rani', 'Hasimkhan Dewan', 'Dhundiy Palwan','Kanchanmala', 'Madhumala', 'Shantikanyar Baromashi', ' Manipurer Larai' etc.* So, it is evident that a treasure of folk literary tradition based on the historical incidents was developed long ago in the region. *'Jangiyar Geet'* or *'Latur Larair gan'*, – the songs or the ballads composed on the events of the Mutiny 1857, commemorate this glorious tradition and inheritance.

The ballad *Jangiyar Geet* is a heroic folk-tale, composed of 1344 lines, complete in form with a regular sequence of events. It is a narrative poetry and has for its subject a single action, beginning with a convincing cause. The attention of the poet does never swerve a bit from the theme he treats of and the story moves speedily towards the end which ultimately rises to a great pathos, poetic excellence and epic grandeur.

The characteristics portrayed in the ballad, however, strike us by the solemn renunciation and the spirit of sacrifice which ultimately leads to an ethical sublimity. The wife of the Subedar of the rebellious army, who has been portrayed as heroine in the ballad bears a majesty of a glorious woman-hood and the capacity of endurance. She sacrificed her life for a noble cause, the cause for which thousands of lives were dedicated in our country in the 'First war of Independence' against the British Raj.

The composition of the narration, its continuation up to the date, factual evidences incorporated within it, the religio-political and economic factors which moulded the psychological and ideological attitude of the people and their reflections in the songs and ballad,— all these clearly reveal the fact that the Mutiny 1857, casted a deep impact on the life of the rural mass of the North-East region, specially Surma- Barak valley.

A thorough scrutiny of the internal evidences provides us with the fact that the songs and the ballad *'Jangiyar Geet'* was primarily composed by a poet after the lapse of few years of the mutiny. It is observed that the attitude of the rebellious force, their activities at Chittagong and their march through the hill tracts of Tripura and Comilla and the unfortunate disaster ultimately they met at Latu and adjoining areas of Sarespur hills near Badarpur, the route they followed and the time and season as it is mentioned in the narration, and even the characters like the zamindar of Langla and the traitor Kalamia of Latu, all these incidents and activities of the characters are corroborated with the recorded evidences. Association of these facts in such an adequate striking manner firmly establish the fact that in the composition of the narration, conscious intellects were very much involved.

It is evident that there are families in the region residing in the Pancha khanda area in the district of Sylhet, now in Bangladesh; Batarashi, Latu, Bagarsangan, Inatpur areas of Karimganj district who claim their ancestry from the fugitive mutineers. In Bagarsangan, in the Holy Mokam, there is a grave of one saint, whom the people of the area identify as the martyrs of the war of Latu which took place at the time of Mutiny on 18th December, 1857.There is a place named as Asimganj in the district of Karimganj, where a nearby Mokam is recognized as a sacred seat of Asim Shah. The people identify him as an associate of the sepoys of the Mutiny. In the Sarespoor hill at Badarpur near the village Jumbasti, on the top of the hillock there is a seat of one Fakir which is recognized as a *'Lal kurta Jangi'*s Mokam. There is an Ashrama on the bank of the river Kusiara, at Bhanga Bazar, near Badarpur which is popularly recognized as *'Lal Babajir Akhra'*. It may be mentioned here that the mutineers of the 34th Native Infantry Regiment of Chittagong were commonly dressed with Red Coats. The Pir Bakhar Shah of Cachar district was also popularly recognized as a warrior of the Sipahi Juddha. He had two scars of bullet wounds in his right arm which the people of the valley had seen. One Jamal Uddin, a retired octogenerian Subedar of the British Force, expressed that one Jalal Uddin Khan who was a Jamadar of the mutinied troops skillfully managed to escape with a small troop in spite of dogged search for his arrest. This Jalal Uddin was a Hindustani Brahmin and later on adopted Islam in order to influence the local Muslims of Cachar district to rise against the British Raj.

Evidences also provide us with the fact that one Sheikh Fakir was arrested by the British force from the rebel troops. The official records too give us the information that there were families of sepoys who managed to escape from the dogged hunting of the British army. It is learnt from Lt Sheror's note that after the Latu encounter the fugitives were scattered into three or four groups and marched towards Cachar in different ways through hills, jungles and riversides. Among them a group of forty to fifty escaped towards the hill range of Badarpur. Recorded evidences also mentioned that the rebel sepoys of 34th Native Infantry Regiment were 300 in numbers. Other than these a large number of convicts of the Jail and other family members including women and children were also with the fugitives. All total 272 numbers of mutineers may be traced out, killed or arrested, the rest took refuge in the different parts of the region. Thus it can easily be understood that behind the composition of this long narrative poetry the possibility of the existence of a person or persons who was or were associates of the mutineers cannot be ruled out. It might have so happened that the sepoys or their followers simply narrated the facts and the village-bards composed the songs with their natural artistic skill and efficiency in local Bengali dialectical form. Other than the poetic and historical value the present narrative possesses within it a resourceful treasure of religio-social and political study. Though the poet of the narrative is a devout follower of Islam, and has portrayed almost all the characters as holy warriors of 'Din', yet his heart is not debased by any narrow ill-bred sentiment of his racial prejudice.

The bard pays his salute to the Pirs and Nabis as well as to the Hindu Deities. The Hymn given in the prologue of the *Geet* undoubtedly establishes the fact that the liberal ideas which generally prevail among the Mohammedan folk-bards and the sense of secularity of their views has also been revealed in the illustrations by the recognition of the Hindu shrines, God and Goddesses, along with their own religious belief and wisdom.

It is thus, with all its characteristics, this ballad–*'Jangiyar Geet'*—'The Songs of the Warriors', of the Mutiny 1857 undoubtedly stands unparallel in the tradition of the folk-literature in Bengal and North-East.

4

The Tale as it was Told: Jangiyar Geet

The story narrated in the ballad Jangiyar Geet[1] is composed of 1344 lines in local Bengali dialect. The translated version in English is of 1165 lines. The content matters are dealt in two parts. The first one relates to the incidents that took place in and around Chittagong, now in Bangladesh. The second part deals with the incidents which follow the entry of the mutineers in the District of Sylhet (now in Bangladesh), and Cachar. The tale begins with a glorious uprise in Chittagong and ends in the tragic defeat in encounters in the vicinity of the hill range of Badarpur, Sarespur and Hailakandi region in Barak Valley.

The recital starts with the salutation to Allah-Nabi, Saraswati and other Hindu god and goddesses. In the 'Hymn' he pays his tribute to the rising sun the benign incarnation of light, - the light which removes all darkness at dawn. But the day is encircled by bad- omen. In the North, he offers his tribute to the Devas of Unakuti[2], who have assembled in a party. In the West, he pays all honour to the Holy Macca and convey his salam to all the people of Hindusthan other than the Hindus. In the South, he offers tribute to the Kaliday sagar[3], where a pelted stone takes six months to reach the bottom of it. Next he tenders all his reverence to Allah and all Nabis. He salutes his Murshid, and all Aulias[4] and all the people who have gathered to listen the songs. Then the singstar bows down to the Goddess Saraswati for her blessings and prays, "Oh mother, it is you who have taken me in your shelter in my early boyhood of twelve years of age and now in this old age of eighty, I hope you will not be unkind to me. If I am deprived from your blessings, you will be the killer of your son Kartika and Ganesha. This way I pay homage to the all corners of the earth. Then I salute at first, Allah-Niranjan, Bibi, Ali, Mother Fatemah, Hasan and Hussain. After that, I tender my salam to all Nabis and Ambiyas. And then I again bow to the feet of my Murshid, my preceptor, parents and all the Hindus and the Muslims who are my brothers. Oh mother Jogini, now be gratuitous to come down and inspire me with songs. I offer my all reverence to you. God knows, what is written in the fate today, still this poor fellow is going to recite the *Heroic tale of the warriors*." After completion of the 'Hymn' the bard then proceeds to narrate the story in a melodious tune, — *'Oh the ordeal of Allah is befalling us.'*

There was a man named Mogal at Nagarpur town near Chittagong. He was serving as a sepoy in the police battalion of the British force. He had five sons and a wife. Hafiz, the youngest one, being educated in Madrasa, came back to the house and informed his father to attend him immediately. Accordingly Mugal returned home from the Headquarter taking leave for a few days. When the father and the sons were in Launch, Hafiz asked his father to resign his service. He tried to convince him by saying that the Police service under the British Govt. is ***'haram'***, a sinful act:

I wished to remind you, father
Koran forbids the service in police,

You have five offsprings by the grace of Allah
Why not stay home and
Work together to earn.
If that's not enough, my father
I'll maintain by begging even,
For Allah's sake, resign the job atonce.[5]

Instantly Mogal reacted at his sayings and warned the boy for his utterings. Immediately he rushed to the Head quarter and reported the attitude of his son to the officer and came back with a troop to arrest the boy. In the mean time Hafiz rushed to the town and brought a suit of police uniform and a rifle from one Khalifa. On the way both father and the son met with an encounter and Hafiz being defeated secretly took refuge in a Chittagong going ship. At early morning at the port of Chittagong, he managed to escape and met one Subedar of the British Army. There in his house the boy received shelter and protection. At Chittagong, while the "Akika"[6] ceremony of the newly born baby of the Subedar was spoilt by one Ingrej Sahib, instantly hostility against the British was sparked off and ultimately the entire dissatisfied troop openly broke out in to rebellion.

On one Friday, the Subedar invited all the Muslim soldiers of the town to celebrate the *'Akika'* ceremony of his baby. The Junior Sahib was not invited to the ceremony for his English birth and Christianity. At this the Sahib felt insulted and became furious. Immediately he rushed to the place where the Subedar and his followers were engaged in the performance of the rituals. Reaching there he ordered the sepoys to come forward with his share. The poor subordinates tried to convince him by every art of appealing to wait up to the period of the mid-day prayer. But his pride and arrogance immediately led him to become offensive. He then charged his horse through the cook- shed and spoilt all the arrangements and returned to the Bungalow. The suddenness of the incident created great resentments among the sepoys.The Subedar, being the subordinate official of the Sahib, helplessly bursted into tears and appealed to the almighty 'Allah' for redress. He tried to manage the situation in a very calm and quite manner. He ordered his fellow sepoys to bury all the spoilt foodstuff and sent them to buy sweets from the market to entertain guests. He did never utter any word against the heinous misdeed of the English Sahib. Rather he was very much alarmed and troubled with anxiety for the reaction of his wife, who was regarded as a mother of all the sepoys of Chittagong, for her amazing behaviour and strong personality. When the Subedar asked his fellow brothers to come forward to take the sweets for her, nobody dared to shoulder the risk. At last an old man agreed and brought the packets of sweet 'sirni'[7] to her home. Looking into the packets, instantly she became angry and after enquiry when she had come to know the details of the savage acts of the Chota Sahib, she furiously bursted out. She treated the cruelty of the Ingrez sahib as a deliberate attack on the religious faith and prestige of the whole community. She raised ***Jihad*** in the name of ***'Iman'*** and ***'Izzat'*** and roared:

Go and tell the Subedar that
His first duty is to protect the sanctity.
Let him stay in disgrace with his men.
I' am going to charge the sahib
And slaughter him, come what may.[8]

She at once proceeded to take action. Keeping the baby in sleep, she rushed with open sword in hand; like the mother goddess Rana rangini Durga:

She furnished herself
With war attire and arma nents.
She landed on the bungalow of the Sahib
Her sword flushed like emerald,
Holding the shield in the left hand
She proceeded towards him.[9]

The woman valiantly jumped on the 'kaffir' and mercilessly cut him into pieces. She finished the whole action dramatically within a few minutes by her brilliant tactfulness. Returning home she summoned one sepoy and directed him to prepare the troops for the rebellion:

Five of you get ready to go with me.
We shall devastate the city of Chittagong
Put on your attire soon.[10]

She roared like a furious tigress and valiantly announced her firm determination. Her courageous act and undaunted spirit inspired all the soldiers of the five units to unite against the atrocities of the Englishmen and their regime.[11] They had the belief that the sacrifice of their lives would be graced by the almighty. The sepoys take oath to fight with their last drop of blood against the intruder British, under the leadership of the Subedar and his valiant wife. They believed that this 'jihad' against the ***'kaffirer jat, nasra Ingrej'***[12] was the will of the almighty. The mother invoked the holy warriors to take revenge against the enemy who defiled Islam. Instantly the brave soldiers of five units jumped on the enemy.

Realising the gravity of the situation, the British authority sent messages to Bartupi for re-enforcement. Fierce fighting was continued for seven days and the holy warriors won the battle in six encounters, but lost the last seventh combat at the field of Rongtuli. Being defeated they plundered the treasury and armoury and took their plight towards north. At first they crossed the river *Feni*[13] and reached to the northern bank and then entered into the hilly track of Tipura. The target of the fugitive was the kingdom of Jayantia, where, they believed that they would get protection and shelter. But the reality was unknown to them that the kingdom had already been annexed to the British.

The marching line of the fugitives was composed of cavalry and infantry. They had their family members with them including other convicts who were imprisoned in the Jail of Chittagong. From Tripura via Comilla they changed their direction towards the north-east. After crossing the hilly tracks they slightly turned towards the north–west and arrived on the foot- hills of the bordering areas of Sylhet district. On the bank of the river *Kuia Khal* they met one Rabai Patni, a fisher man with a fishing net on his shoulder. In the meantime the messages were communicated by the Chittagong authority to all concerned to search out and arrest the mutineers.

The ***mother,*** the wife of the subedar, frankly narrated their alarmed condition and the entire affairs of Chittagong to Rabai Patni and prayed for shelter and food for the day:

We're Muslims, we've escaped from
The city of Chittagong,
Please help us, for the English savages
Chasing from behind.[14]

Being convinced Rabai promised to provide them food and protection. Then he went to observe the situation. Within a few minutes he noticed that a large number of troops were advancing along the road. He then rushed forward and came down near the river side, far away from the fugitives and pretended to catch fishes with his net. The searchers then approached to Rabai and enquired whether he had found any troop to flee away in this direction. In reply, Rabai admitted that he had seen such a force to take plight towards the hill range of eastern direction. The soldiers hurriedly rushed chasing the fugitives following the false path as directed by Rabai. He then came back cautiously on the river side and engaged himself in catching fishes till the entire force disappeared from the sight. In the meantime he directed his sons to make adequate arrangements to entertain all the members of the fugitive force at his house. Being pleased with his hospitality one member of the force converted Rabai and his family into Islam. –

> *On that occasion*
> *Along with Rabai all the fishermen of the place*
> *Embraced the new faith, and dined.*[15]

Next morning the mutineers reached at ***Langla,*** a renowned place in the district of Sylhet. There the influential muslim Zamindar[16] offered them cordial hospitality. In the meantime the sepoys of the Sylhet Light Infantry spotted them. Being alarmed they rushed towards the eastern direction leaving behind the half–cooked meal. On the way they looted the market of the Zamindar which was opened to them. In hungry and panicy they procured whatever they found eatables. They took jungle roots, berries, garden vegetables, fruits, and leaves. In this way they crossed ***Kulaura***[17] and arrived at a village named ***Khan Bahadurer Par***[18] after a long march for three days. There in the house of one ***Nabab Mia,***[19] a Zamindar of that locality, the mutineers took shelter and food peacefully for a day. At dusk they once again embarked upon their journey towards ***Latu Bazar.***[20]

Early in the morning they arrived at Latu and searched

out the Muslim Zamindar ***Kalamia*** [21]at his house. They belived that the cause for which they were fighting was the common cause of all the Muslims of the country. Accordingly they sought shelter and protection of Kalamia. But this Muslim Zamindar played the traitor. He received them in his house with a false cordiality in order to keep them under surveillance. He then surreptitiously slept out and went to the river side and found the sepoys of the British force who were in search of the fugitives. He then loudly drew their attention and inform the news of the arrival of the mutineers and bargained for his loyal service.–

Have you seen the warriors here around?
'What will be my reward, if I
Tell you the truth?
'Oh, be assured, we promise you
the lordship of this place,
the market of Latu all will be your.
'Do come here crossing the river
I assure you hundred rupees,
Take a small boat and come near.[22]

The sepoys then hurriedly arrived at the house of Kalamia and observed the number and position of the mutineers from a long distance and rushed to inform the authority. When traitor Kalamia tried to entrap and arrest them secretly, the helpless mother fervently appealed to the Almighty Allah for redress. Suddenly terrible storm came down, uprooted the large trees and utterly ruined the house of Kalamia. The fugitives took the blessings from the Heaven and managed to escape from the grips of Kalamia and took refuge on the deep jungles of Malegarh hillock.

The thirsty mother then after a long period of journey

went down towards the bank of the river with arm guards and opened the haversack where in the baby was tied up on her flight. In the mean time the baby was passed away unawares and turned into a stiff mass of human flesh. The poor mother with the decomposed baby in her arms bursted into tears. In the mean time the sepoys of the British force surrounded them and opened fire on the river side. The mother was killed on the spot. The fugitives hurriedly performed the rituals of the burial ceremony of the baby and the wife of the Subedar on the Malegarh Mokam and engaged in encounter.

Soon a fierce fight took place at Latu. The mutineers tried to gain over the enemy by every art of appealing to their religious feelings as well as nationality. It may be mentioned that all the sepoys of the Sylhet Light Infantry were Hindusthanies. Falling this they taunted them by calling 'Nasra Ingreser Kuttas and golams', but in reply they received only bullets. In this encounter several numbers of mutineers died martyr's death and seventeen were arrested. The remaining took flight towards the east and the south- eastern directions.

To the east of Latu Market place the arrested seventeen sepoys were tied with a large tree and shot to death. They bravely embraced the glorious death. This tree is still there as a witness to that incident. The graveyard of Malegarh Tila bears the memory of this valiant out-break. The recital narrates this defeat in a melodious tune:

Oh, the warriors
The Jangiyas bewail
In their tryst,
Feeding on the wild grass;

The Subedar bahadur, again, bewail
For the Holy faith.[23]

The fugitives then fled away through the villages of ***Pathu,***[24] ***Bedrong,***[25] ***Barapara,***[26] ***Maizgram***[27] and then arrived at ***Bishkut.***[28] The Zamindar ***Suruzmia***[29] of that locality coldly refused to give the rebels any shelter. They repeatedly appealed to his consense in the name of religion as well as nationality, but Suruzmia paied no heed to their words, rather he betrayed them. Then Subedar requested him to show the path towards Bishkut so that they could took their plight to Jayantia. They had no idea about the location of the village and that they were already in Bishkut, that fact was unknown to them.

Jayantia Kingdom is only two days journey on foot from Bishkut. But Suruzmia dissuaded him by saying that Bishkut was too far away and they crossed only on *'kut'*[30] from Chittagong, nineteen more 'kuts' were to be covered till they might reach Bishkut. At this, being frustrated they took their flight towards the East and crossed ***'Anair haor',***[31] a plain and marshy track between Karimganj and Badarpur. The season was of producing Rabi crops. The period of the journey was the month of December. The linseeds were growing ripening throughout the field. While they crossed the track, they procured handful of the seeds, to meet hunger. In return they compensated the loss of the grower by depositing money throughout the field under the earthen clods. The bard in tearful eyes laments:

The hungry warriors now crossed Bishkut
And landed on Anair haor,
They are tired beyond measure
And incapable of moving a step further.

[Oh, Allah, the Jangiyas bewail.]

they walked through the Anair haor
and entered into the field of grains,
they picked up leaves of linseeds
and had their fill with it.[32]

In this way they arrived at the east of the Haor and there they met one old man. Asking him they came to know the name and the address of the Muslim landlord of this locality, one Golam Rabbani Chowdhury. There in the house of the Zamindar they were cordially welcomed and offered food and shelter. At dusk they again started their journey towards the foothills of Saraspoore. In the meantime the British troops encircled them in the hill and opened fire. In this encounter the mutineers met their tragic end. The Subedar along with many other comrades died a heroic death. The remaining fugitives fled- away hitherto.

NOTES

1. Jang, means war. *Jangiyar Geet* means the song of the warriors.
2. A famous seat of the God Shiva and his associates in Tripura.
3. The name of a mythical sea.
4. Followers of Hazrat Shah Jalal, see Appendix E.
5. Quoted lines from the ballad, 145- 152.
6. A ritual performs after the birth of a new born child by the Muslims.
7. An oblation of sweets offered to deities or to the spirits.
8. Quoted lines, 396-400.
9. *Ibid.*, 405-410.
10. *Ibid.*, 458-460.
11. The letter addressed to the Commander 34th Native Infantry Regiment, Barrackpur by the Magistrate of Chittagong, dated Dec. 24, 1857, confirmed the incidents and the attitudes that followed.— "It appears from all I can gather that a large

feast was given the day before the mutiny, and that all the sepoys were presented at the entertainment, and that they met to talk over the plans for carrying out the mutiny the following day." [Chattagram District Collector's Records, Vol, 259, letters No., 515.]

12. *Kaffir*, the Infidels.
    Nasra, the non believers (according to Islam)
13. A river name in Chittagong.
14. Quoted lines, 646-649.
15. *Ibid.*, 693-695.
16. This Zamindar was Gouch Ali Khan, the grandfather of Ali Amzad Khan, a legendary personality of Sylhet district.
17. A trade center and an important Railway Junction in the district of Sylhet.
18. A place on the foot hills of Patharia forest range.
19. An wealthy person.
20. A big market place and the Revenue collection centre.
21. A ryot of the Zamindar of Pratapgarh Pargana, and after the mutiny he was rewarded for his loyal service to the British.
22. Quoted lines, 834-842.
23. *Ibid.*, 1007-1012.
24. A village south west of Karimganj.
25. A village name.
26. A village near the river Langai.
27. A village name.
28. A village of historical importance.
29. A land holder.
30. *Kut*, a measurement of length or distance of 20 miles.
31. A plain and marshy track between Karimganj and Badarpur.
32. Quoted lines, 1083-1090.

5

Mutiny: Its Impact and the People of Surma-Barak

In his first dispatch, dated June 10, 1857, R. Stewart wrote, "the popular mind in Cachar seems in no way affected by the disturbances which are occurring in the North West.'[1] But when the news of the march of the mutinied sepoys towards Cachar was received by him he was somewhat alarmed and expressed his apprehension in his letter dated December 7,1857, that the fugitive Manipuri Princes residing in Cachar might take advantage of the situation. On December 26, he informed, 'the people of the district are much alarmed, the Bengalees being in the greatest of fear'. In the same letter he again expressed anxiety over the possible alliance between the Manipuries and the rebel sepoys. On January 13, 1858, he intimated the actual involvement of a Manipuri Prince and his followers with the mutineers. In the same letter it was also reported that three sepoys were taken prisoners by the villagers. Three days later he wrote, "as it is now apparent that portion of our own subjects in this district are on rebellion against the Government."[2] This assertion is quite contrary to his earlier contention. Unfortunately Stewart did not give any detailed information to the identification of these subjects. Probably there were some other groups of people whom he targeted. Otherwise he would not have sought for special power under Act XI of 1837 for trial of such sympathizers.[3]

Stewart made a detail report to the authorities suggesting preventive measures for future security of the district. Though by this time the mutiny was over but he thought it necessary to draw preemptive plans because by that time some more report received by him made him apprehensive of the situation. In his report he took cognizance of a statement given by one of his Scout who was captured and imprisoned by the mutineers in their camp, which runs as follows, "That after recruiting themselves at Luckipoor, the mutineers joined by the Munnipoorie population who were all prepared to assist, and possibly by the Hindustani sepoys among our own troops, should return to the station, loot the treasury and the Magazine, and made themselves master of the country.'[4]

Prince Narindrajit Singh who joined with the mutineers was apprehended in Manipur while on his flight towards Manipur with severe wound after the struggle that occurred in Binnakandi. Stewart demanded his immediate surrender and wrote a letter to the Political Agent to send him in his custody for trial. The prince was the first cousin of the Raja Chandra Kirti Singh and Stewart was suspicious about the treatment of the Raja of Manipur and anxiously solicited authorities instructions and wrote, "although (Narindrajit) seriously opposed him (Raja of Manipur), being himself a claimant to the throne, still I anticipate that it will be with some reluctance that the Raja will give him up to suffer the punishment which is his due."[5] Stewart had also given importance to the geographical location of the Cachar and made the authorities aware of the fact that the region was surrounded by the hostile tribes like Nagas and Lushais. He categorically emphasized that on these tribes, "no reliance is to be placed."[6]

All these official versions provide us with the fact that the prime concern of the authority was the Manipuri Princes and their followers. Secondly, at a later stage Stewart was uneasy with the attitude of some members of his own troops. And finally, he was also apprehensive of the possible hostilities of the frontier tribes.

It is significant that nowhere in his dispatches Stewart expressed any concern for the attitude of the common masses of Cachar plains. At times he did mention one or two zaminders and their agents but he was more or less sure of the allegiance of the common people of the district besides the Manipuris.

Thus it is apparent that his sources or Kuki scouts did not report him anything adverse in this respect. Now the question is, was the authority correct in their assessment of the mode and attitude of the common people? From the recorded official history we find nothing to contest Stewart's opinion. But if we go through the oral tradition, the secondary source of re-creating history from below, and analyze, it will be clearly understood that the great Mutiny 1857, imprinted a positive influence on the people of the region. Evidently, it is observed that the common mass did not directly involved themselves in the mutiny but psychologically they shared their cause. They did not take arms as because they were not an organized force but they raised their loud voice and expressed their anguish mood against the atrocities of the British Imperial power which was surely a mightier power than any militant force. Since the period of transfer of Dewani of Bengal to the East India Company in 1765 up to the Mutiny 1857, if we analyse the incidents that took place on different occasions and the peoples participation and reactions, it is evident that the people of this region, particularly, the southern part of Assam traditionally bear the role against the foreign rule. This region is widely known for its anti British movements. Events like the Muharram massacre of 1781; the Revolt of Nawab Radharam of 1786; Ganga Singh's rebellion of 1789; insurrection of Aga Muhammad Reza of 1799, Civil disobedience of 1811 all these evidently prove that the people of the region were hostile against the supremacy of the British power prior to the Mutiny 1857. Other than these, the attitude of the British colonial approach towards the king of Jaayantia, Cachar, and Manipur and their relation with the other hill tribes of the North East was looked upon with utter dissatisfaction by the different sections.

The malicious act of the British in respect of the trade and management of which they were partners, obviously created strong resentments in the Valley. The unholy alliance of the authority with a section of the people like land holders, Mahajanas and other vested interest groups was seriously noticed by the common mass. The introduction of English replacing Persian as a court language and the new education policy adopted by the Govt. made the people, mainly Muslims, furious. Pride and arrogance of the British even led them to consider natives of the country an under serving the name of human beings at that time. These attitudes hurt the Muslims in general who for centuries past received special privileges and enjoyed immunities. And these Muslims played a vital role in the anti British movement since the Battle of Plassey to the freedom movement.

The western portion of the Surma valley forming the Sylhet sarkar of Bengal Subah automatically came under East

India Company in 1765 with the transfer of Dewani of Bengal, Bihar and Orissa. But the territory of Cachar and Jayantia remained independent. These two kingdoms were subsequently annexed to the British power in the year 1832 and 1835 respectively. The grant of Dewani of Bengal by Shah Alam II, the Mughal emperor to Robert Clive, secured for the East India Company, "the suprintendncy of all lands and the collection of all revenues."[7] At that period the eastern most boundary of the Raj was up to the border of present district of Karimganj and Cachar. At first the administration of the district of Sylhet was under Dacca Council. In order to make it easy to Govern, in 1771, Samner was deputed to Sylhet as the Supervisor. In this period the primary duty of the supervisor of the Company was the collection of revenues and the judiciary power was entrusted with the Subedar.[8]

In 1772 Macpeace Thackery, the grandson of Mr.Thackery the eminent novelist of England, was posted there as the collector.[9]

The Company, at that period was much interested with their profits of the business. This region is resourceful for its Limestone, forest products, elephants, paddy and other perfumery goods since time immemorial.[10]

From ancient times the trade of Limestone was a most profitable one and the company made a treaty with the Nawab Mir Kasim in 1762 in the following terms and conditions that, "one half of chunam purchased by the Gomastahs of the company from the people for the Government at the customary rate of the places the tenants and inhabitants of the district shall receive no injury."[11] But when the authority came to realize the fact that the actual gain was more than their assessment they tried to exert all powers to harvest their fortunes. In the meantime the Dewani was transferred to the Company and they concentrated their all attentions to earn money. It is observed that at the time of Thackery, annually one Lakh twenty thousand mounds of limestone was exported to Calcutta from Sylhet. In later period, it was recorded that in the year 1902-1903 twenty-lakh mounds of limestone was exported from Sylhet. At that time the rate of the limestone was Rs. 35.00 per hundred mounds. It is also seen in the period of Thackery that, for obvious reasons the Zamindars of Baniya Chung and Khalijuri reacted against foreign traders and the authority had to apply force to manage the situation.[12]

At that period King Chatra Singh of Jayantia attacked the trading boats on the river Surma and consequently the territory was invaded by the British.[13] Thackery also earned huge amount from the export- trade of elephants, and other illegal sources like black –marketeerings, hoardings etc. Unlawful salt- deal and profit motive led him into troubles with the local traders and ultimately he was removed from the district. Narrating the profit earning motive and the meanness of the British officers, Edmond Burke rightly comments that, "Neither a reseal nor a pattern of virtue, they were full grown in fortune long before they were ripe in principle."[14]

After Thackery, Holland came to Sylhet in 1776, and raised the target of the collection of the revenue of the district upto two and half lakhs annually. This act created great resentment among the different sections of the people. Though Holland finished his business successfully yet he did not forget to state that the people were most turbulent and much troubles had to face to realize the revenues.[15] He was then succeeded by Robert Lindsaye in the year 1778. Assuming the charge of the collector he confidently managed the problems and was successful in collecting the revenues. But he also had to face serious troubles in his period of administration. As a repurcuson of the British administration the events that took place in his tenure of service in the district created a large scale massacre. The impact of these incidents ultimately made the people hostile against the British Raj. Among these the remarkable events are the 'Khasi rebellion' in 1779, the 'Muharram Massacre' in 1781 and the 'Revolt of Nawab Radharam' in 1786.

It is evident that in Muslim rule, particularly in Nawabi Amal, the peace and amity among the different sections of the people in Sylhet was never seriously disturbed. Both the Hindus and the Muslims were honored in the court and they enjoyed equal rights. The priestly Hindu castes, even in 1810 A.D. received land grants from the Muslim Fauzdars of Sylhet.[16] In fact fauzdars were still powerful up to that period. The collectors of the Company became all-powerful in later period. After the transfer of Dewani economic conditions and the balance of power quickly changed to a different angle and a new administrative and wealthy class emerged. The Muslims who enjoyed all privileges in their regime became frustrated and naturally a sense of hostility against the British and the loyal Hindus was developed. Dewan Manik Chand of Sylhet, whose ancestors enjoyed special privileges in the Nawabi Amal became loyal to the British for vested interests. It is observed that when Manik Chand was charged with a suit by Durlav Das, a wealthy landlord and trader of salt, the authority pleaded in favour of the Dewan.[17] For the unfair association with Mr. Holland, he also earned serious dissatisfactions of the people in revenue matters. In the report of Holland to John Hogarth, the acting chief of co-provincial council of revenue, Dacca, stated as such. "Manik Chand the Dewan of this place being obliged to repair to Dacca in order to find bail and answer to a suit commenced against him by one Dullab Das in the Supreme Court of indicators. I have taken up on myself the charge of transacting the minutes of the business of this province till his return."[18]

The people, particularly Muslims, gradually became hostile with the Raj and their associates, and in 1781, they openly broken into rebellion with an intention to expel the foreign powers from the country. The Hindus, being alarmed, reported the matter to Lindsaye earlier. But he did not take it seriously. On the auspicious day of Muharram the Muslims attacked the temple of the Dewan Manikchand and created havocs in the town. They heavily ransacked the houses of Hindus and wounded them in large numbers.The report of atrocities from the different localities was reported to Lindsaye and he immediately rushed to the place of occurrence. After arrival he found the large gathering of about three hundred armed Muslims on the spot. He then, requested one Pirjada, the leader of the rebel to withdraw his men from the place and assured him to provide with justice. But he did not show any regard to his words rather attacked him. Narrating the incident Lindsaye states, "He immediately draw his sword, and exclaiming with a loud voice, ***'This is the day to kill or die. The reign of the English is at an end'***, and aimed a heavy blow at my head."[19] Lindsaye instantly resisted the attack and fired his pistol and Pirjada died on the spot. In the mean time the sepoys charged the mob and dispersed them. The rebels retreated with heavy causalties. One jamadar died and twelve other sepoys of the company were injured. It is also learnt from the report of Lindsaye submitted to Hastings, the Governor General and Members of the Supreme Council, Fort William, Calcutta, that the authority was apprehensive of the Muslim desperadoes.

Lindsaye also expressed his concern about the Muslims and stated that they were more unmanageable and turbulent than the timid Hindus.[20]

Though Lindsaye was satisfied with his actions and was confident that, 'the most turbulants are no more', yet the Muslims did not forget the assault. A few days later, a Fakir sought permission to meet Lindsaye with a false plea. But his intentions made Hamilton suspicious and the man was arrested. To avoid assault, Fakir then committed suicide.[21]

One Syedullah, whose father Pirjada was killed in the Muharram massacre, also went out to take revenge against Lindsaye. At the time of Muharram incidents he was a teen-aged boy and witnessed the consequence of his father and from that day he promised to retaliate the acts of Lindsaye. After long years, Syedullah then attained his maturity, and Lindsaye settled down in London after his retirement. One day Syed left Sylhet for England in search of the murderer of his father. In London he took shelter in the house of Mr. Small whom he met in the ship in his voyage. Mr. Small was a neighbour of Lindsaye. One day Syedullah desperately made an attempt and entered into the house of Lindsaye with a firm determination to kill him but could not stand before his affectionate personality and ultimately he surrendered.[22] These incidents definitely indicate how the Muslims reacted against the British rule.

The revolt of Nawab Radharam a local Hindu Chief of Pratapgarh Pargana, against the Government also provide us with the intentions and attitude of the people towards the British. Radharam came in the region in search of fortune and setteled in Pratapgarh Pargana where the present Patharkandi and Ratabari towns of Karimganj district are situated. There he came along with a Fakir named Saija

Badshah and became his disciple. Gradually he over powered the local tribal chiefs and made them loyal. He made a treaty with the king of Tripura and became all powerful in the south-eastern part of Sylhet and denounced the supremacy of the Foreign-rule. He stopped the payment of revenue to the authorities, and declared himself as an independent Nawab.

In the month of November,1786, Radharam attacked the chowki of the government at Chargola and killed many subjects of the Company.[23] Immediately Lindsaye the collector of Sylhet, sent troops under Lt. Davidson to resist Radharam. The authority also ordered the Zamindars of Pratapgarh, Jafargarh and Egarsati Pargana to assist the Company's force against Radharam. It is also learnt from the report of the collector, that the Company was seriously concerned about the collection of revenue for the disturbance. The government force attacked the territory of Radharam, gutted his houses. They also looted money, plundered the cattles and heavily ransacked the houses of the people who were loyal to the enemy. In his report Allen stated that "Mr. Lindsaye promptly dispatched some sepoys to the place with instructions to burn the villages of Radharam's people and lift his cattles."[24] Radharam immediately fortified his force in nearby hills on the bank of the great lake Sonbil. Subsequently in two encounters British forces were defeated, but ultimately Radharam lost the third. The troubles continued for five months.[25] Kanuram Choudhury, a Zamindar of Pratapgarh, who was an intimate friend of Radharam; and Golam roja Choudhury, another Zamindar of the locality, betrayed the Nawab and with their help the Company succeeded to drive out the rebels.[26]

It may be recalled here that this Choudhury family of Pratapgarh helped the British at the period of Mutiny 1857.[27]

Radharam at last took refuge in the hill-tracts and ultimately was arrested at Siddeswar, on the bank of the river Barak near Badarpur in a holy fair (Baruni Mela). While he was imprisoned in an Iron-cage and was transported to Sylhet, on the way he committed suicide in the river Surma.

Robert Lindsaye, was then succeeded by John Willis. In his period Zamindar Ganga Singh of Barakhia attacked the territories of Khasi tribes and compelled the subjects of 22 villages to pay him the revenues. He then declared himself as an independent king and stopped paying revenue to the Company. In order to establish his supremacy he attacked the Police Station of Icchamati and plundered the market. He also took the control over the trade route in Surma river between Chhatak and Sunamganj. He also killed all the members of the family of one Baru Roy, a close relative of him and an informer of the East India Company. The authority became alarmed and attacked Ganga Singh with artillery and infantry. In a pitched battle in 1790 the Company defeated him and on the way of transportation to Calcutta he committed suicide in the river Padma.[28]

In 1799, Aga Muhammad Reza, an Iranian Muslim, attacked Cachar and made himself master of the country declared himself as the Twelfth Imam and took arms against the East India Company in order to free India from the yoke of the British power. He attacked the Company's thana at Bundasil at Badarpur. Subedar Kalyan Singh was successful to arrest Reza and seized five numbers of cannons and ninety sepoys of the rebel troops. Shortly afterwards Kalyan Singh with other disgruntled sepoys, who were discharged from the Company's troops, occupied Hailakandi area of Cachar. The King of Cachar appealed to the Magistrate of Sylhet and subsequently the authority was succeeded in expelling the adventurer.[29]

In 1811, at Sylhet the people became furious with the authority and openly came out to protest against the decision of the imposition of taxes on the 1092 number of house-holdings. They resisted the collectors and had shut-down the doors of all the business houses on protest.[30] In a sense that was the first instance of civil disobedience in the region, and perhaps in the country against the Raj.

The recorded evidences thus provide us with the fact that the people of different sections of this region from feudal land-holders, Zamindars to traders, and the local chiefs to the mass all became hostile with the foreign rule since the transfer of Dewani.The aggrieved classes also ridiculed the loyal vested interested class. The common people till today commemorate the role of his ancestors who raised their voice and arms against the colonial rule and sing popular folk songs which were composed by unknown village bard on the glorious incidence of uprise and struggles.

The villagers of Pratapgarh Pargana remember the heroic zeal and the bravery of Nawab Radharam with honour and curiosity. The people of that period were influenced by his glorious activities and inspired with the sentiment of patriotism. To commemorate these events and to satisfy the need of the time, the bards composed lyrical songs in verses, which is popularly known as ***'Jay Mangaler Geet'***. Jay Mangal was the eldest son of Radharam who after the defeat of his father, wandered from hill to hill, village to village, for shelter and protection. Ultimately he was arrested. The pathos of the narrative deeply touches the mind and the heart and momently fills with woes and sufferings of the braves. The songs reveal the sentiment of the people in support of the revolt. They, particularly, the degenerated untouchable cremators and other marginalized class cried all around, and promised to rebuild the houses of Jay Mangal which were brutally devastated by the British soldiers, if he could return back to home.[31] We have also observed at the fall of Jayantia kingdom how the people expressed their resentment in folk songs against the foreign domination.

From all these evidences it is observed that the people were very much concerned with the British administration from the very beginning and expressed their sorrows and anguish in their traditional forms and means long before the mutiny period. So it was evident that the struggle for freedom 1857 and its theme would cast a deep impact on the popular mind and the response of the mass towards these soul stirring patriotic incidents was for obvious reasons commemorated in the heroic folk ballad 'Jangiyar geet'. In fact within the exciting period of the mutiny the sentiment of the people of the region and their society took a new birth towards the national spirit and wisdom.

Besides this ballad there are innumerable stray songs composed by unknown village bards on the theme drawn from exciting events of the struggle. These are popularly known as *'Latur Larair gan'*,—the songs of the war of Latu or *'Sipahi Juddher geet'*. These songs are also the evidences of the fact that the people in different areas of the region reacted equiovocally in the same time with same spirit and in a same tune. A few excerpts of such songs, composed in local Bengali dialect of Sylhet-Cachar are run like this:

(a) *'Jainga aila re Latur pantha diya*
tare dekhiya angrej bhage
Jainta pahar giya,
Latur larait mari gela kata hay re hay
darja mara taratari dhari niba nay'.[32]

— the sepoys have marched along the road of Latu, seeing them the English soldiers take their flight towards Jayantia hills.

Oh! innumerables are died in the fight of Latu. Shut the door immediately, otherwise they will capture you.

(b) *'Jaio na jaio na bhai re*
Latur bazaar diya,
Sho e sho e sipai aichain
Angrej khediya, hae re
Angrej khediya'.[33]

— Oh brother, do not go by the bazaar of Latu, the sepoys have marched in hundreds, chasing the Englishmen.

(c) *'Duar bandha- re sipahi aila ghate*
Saheb babu- e hukum dila
Morba- ey fansir kathe
Hai- re morba- ey fansir kathe'.[34]

— Oh brother, shut your door, the sepoys are all around. The Sahib has given order, you will be hanged, if you give them shelter.

(d) *'Oh, man paran fate- re*
chakshe dekha day-e
kalir kope hai hai
sipair paran ja-e
pathe basi kande sati
patir ashay-e
putra kanya asahay-e
kare hay-e hay-e'.[35]

— Oh! my heart laments at the sight. Alas! at the omen of dark age, the lives of the sepoys are facing tragic death. The wives are crying on the roadsides in search of their husband, hopefully for their return. Oh! the children are also crying helplessly.

There in the village area of Mohanpur, in the district of Hailakandi, the bards sing the popular narrative song of *'Jangir Larair geet'*,[36] the theme of which is similar to that of the ballad ' Jangiyar Geet'.

Besides the official versions and recorded history these evidences of the folk-songs, tales and ballads on 1857, all constitute a very valuable source material in formulating the appropriate history. Though these are not always reliable for historical details yet these are very important to assess the political experiences, attitude and aspirations of the common people.

NOTES

1. Choudhury, Sujit (edt.): *The Mutiny Period in Cachar,* Silchar, 1981, Despatch of R. Stewart to the Secretary, Government of Bengal, Fort William, dated Cachar, June 10, 1857, p. 2.
2. *Ibid.,* Despatches of R. Stewart, dated, Jan. 16, 1858.
3. *Ibid.,* Despatches of R. Stewart, dated, Jan. 16, 1858.
4. *Ibid.,* Despatches of R. Stewart dated, Jan. 16, 1858.
5. *Ibid.,* Despatches of R. Stewart, dated, Jan. 2, 1858.
6. *Ibid.,* Despatches of R. Stewart, dated, Feb. 20, 1858.
7. Bhattacharjee, J.B: *Cachar under British Rule in North-East India,* New Delhi, 1977, p. 19.
8. Ali, Sayed Murtaza: *Hazarat Shahjalal O Sylheter Itihas,* Dacca, 1965, p. 110.
9. *Ibid.,* p. 110.
10. *Ibid.,* p. 112.
11. *Ibid.,* p. 102.
12. *Ibid.,* p. 110.
13. *Ibid.,* p. 153.

14. *Ibid.*, p, 114. Quoted from *Sylhet: Thackary,* by F.B. Brawdly Bist i.c.e.
15. Choudhury, Achyut Charan: *Srihatter Itibritta*, Calcutta, 1917, Vol. II, pt. V., p. 4.
16. Ali, Sayed Murtaza: *op.cit.*, p. 103. Quoted from *Sylhet Thackary* by F.B. Brawdly.
17. Choudhury, Achyut Charan.: *op.cit.*, p. 5.
18. *Ibid.*, Quoted from *'Lives of Lindsaye', Srihatter Itibritta*, Vol. II, pt.v, p. 6.
19. *Ibid.*, p. 18.
20. *Ibid.*, p. 20.
21. *Ibid.*, p. 22.
22. *Ibid.*, p. 27.
23. Allen, B.C.: *Assam District Gazetteer*, Shillong, 1906, Vol.II (Sylhet), p. 41.
24. *Ibid.*, p. 42.
25. Ali, Sayed Murtaza: *op.cit.*, p. 128.
26. Choudhury, Achyut Charan.: *op.cit.*, p. 211.
27. *Ibid.*, p. 51.
28. Ali, Sayed Murtaza.: *op.cit.*, p. 134.
29. Banerjee, A.C.: *Eastern Frontier of British India*, Calcutta, 1946, p. 23.
30. Ali, Sayed Murtaza: *op.cit.*, p. 134.
31. A few lines of the folk songs, Jay Mangaler Geet, composed in the local Bengali dialect, run as follows:

    'Kande re chargolar lok desdesantar
    Jaymangal asiba jabe tahar nagar
    Dom charale milia re banaiya dimu ghar.

    — Quoted from Choudhury, Achyut Charan, *Srihatter Itibritta,* Vol., II, p. 211.
32 Kar, Subir: Personal collection from Basanta Kumar Das an octogenerian village bard of Fakira Bazar, district Karimganj.
33. Bhattacharjee, Jayanta Bhusan: *Mutiny in Cachar, A Survey of the Local Sources.'* Proceedings of North–East India History Asociation, Barapani, Shillong, 1983, p. 21.
34. *Ibid.*
35. *Ibid.*

36. The Folk ballad *Jangir Larair Geet,* the songs of the war of the Mutineers, was collected from the village bards namely, Promod Chandra Das, aged eighty, Naresh Chandra Das, aged eighty five and Md. Ramjan Ali, aged seventy five years. They are the residents of the Mohan Pur Mauza in the district of Hailakandi and primarily belong to the cultivator class.

6

Socio-Religious Aspects of the Ballad

The heroic tale 'Jangiyar Geet' may be treated as an interesting source material for socio -religious study of the region. It is the striking feature of the ballad that the poet or poets, and the listeners for whom it is intended, are all rural mass. Primarily, majority of them are agriculturists and belong to Namasudra, Jele, Patni and other depressed castes of the Hindu society and Muslim backward communities. As a rule the bards are illiterate and uneducated as we understand but not at all less conscious. They have learnt their lessons from the nature and various phenomena of the life and the society. They have developed their tradition of culture from observation and experiences through ages. The teachings of religion moulds their morality and ideas about life. As these war songs are composed for the folk and by the folk, it is obvious that the psychological and ideological approach of the people will be reflected towards the various aspects of life. As the religion played a vital role in the Mutiny 1857,and the songs, as these were composed on that very historical incidents, it is evident that the religious sentiments and attitudes reflected to a greater extent in the development of the story.

The clarion-call to come forward and stand united under the banner of emancipation from the fray yoke is surcharged with an emotion which is attuned with a note of religious overtone. The mass mind is thus provoked with an inspired touch in the name of the 'Din' to rise to the occasion,—

'Wake up my sons wake up and
Take arms in your hands,
The muslims are in great danger
in the tyranny of the infidels.

Ride on the horse back and
Proceed towards the war field
The Almighty is gracious
The enemy will have a fit.

The brave lady heralded her men
In the name of Allah,
Her clarion call assembled all
The sepoys of five battalion.'[1]

The tale of this folk ballad composed in verse form has a dramatic setting. As this ballad is quite distinct from folk-songs of nature and love, and where there is neither the leisure nor the mood to stand and stars at the beauty of nature or delve deep into the sole self, the 'Geet' exhibits a dramatic speed and emotion-charged action and for obvious reason there is no lyrical portion of any considerable length. No poetic fancy but only the grim truth is its beauty. It emphasizes more on the realistic attitude towards the confrontation and sufferings of the life that emerged from a socio- religious and political problems of the Indian National history. The characters and the personalities mentioned in the narrative and the heroic march of the disgruntled rebellious troops through the villages, hills and jungles or the 'haors', swamps and rivers, all bear the definite stamps of the geographical region.

To the common mass the great warriors were never a marauding force or restless wandering band and they never caused any danger to the people. Even they did never lose their dignity of character in the most crucial circumstances. Though the government and its agencies tried utmost to create horror and hostility against the mutineers by distributing pamphlets and adopting various means of publicity, yet the folk acknowledged the *Jangis'* stand and lamented for their tragic end.

The Subedar and his wife and hundreds of other rebellious soldiers had to leave behind their peaceful abode of love and pleasure and march through the frawns of nature and showering of bullets from the enemy camps. In hunger, they had to beg from village to village for shelter and food. They suffered terribly but never surrendered to the 'Nasra Ingrez'. This ballad is rather a prosaic in presentation with descriptive accounts of the wills and woes of the fighting troops.

There is however an under-current of patriotic fervour and heroic zeal. The tragedy of the brave patriots and the sequel of their enthusiasm can be better conceived than expressed.

The mother, the wife of the Subedar, took the assault of the English Sahib seriously and felt insulted. She treated the cruelty of the Ingrez as a deliberate attack on the religious faith and prestige of the whole community. She raised Zihad in the name of ***'Iman'*** and ***'Izzat'***. To her, the primary duty of a man was to protect the sanctity and prestige of the family.

Keeping the baby in sleep, she rushed with open swords in hands and valiantly jumped on the 'Kaffir' and mercilessly killed him. Then she summoned one sepoy and directed him to prepare the troops for the rebellion. She roared like a furious tigress and loudly announced her firm determination.

When the rebellious spirit of the troops picked momentum, she kept herself confined in her room with an intension to judge the role of the Subedar in this crucial juncture. Being a woman, she was well aware of her limitations. In the meantime Subedar plundered the armoury and joined her. He and his wife jointly led the rebel force against the enemy. The mother played the vital role in the seven pitched battles at Chittagong. At last they had to retreat and took flight towards the hilly tract of Chittagong and arrived at Langla in the District of Sylhet via Comilla after a long march. Up to the incidents of Latu massacre, the wife of the Subedar was the central character of the tale. The towering grandeur dignified and self controlled conviction and determination, the spirit of self sacrifice and glorious woman-hood has given her a position to a higher sphere,- that of a heroine of the heroic tale—'Jangiyar Geet'.

The mother is not only the mother of the baby only. She is the mother of all the members of the rebellious force. Her sons, the jangis, never raise any question on her activities; rather they owe their allegiance to her fest with love and regard. Traditional morality, religious prejudice, devotion towards the cause and tremendous personality have given her a grandeur, and side by side motherly compassions make her true idol of a woman.

The theme of the ballad itself unfolds a scene of life-drama, - a drama of patriotic fervors, a "charge of the light Brigade". The warriors were a weaker force in comparison with their enemies, but in morality, character and determinations they were more powerful than the latter. When in action the might of the rebellious force felt helpless, the poet submitted to the supernatural powers. The Holy-warriors were honuored and treated as *'Mumin Musalmans'*, and blended with religious power and might. As it is a creation and recreation of the folk, it thus provide us with the fact that the common people too shared the misfortune of the warriors, and the persons who betrayed their cause, were looked upon by them as traitor and enemy. This way the poet has presented us an interesting and touching story in this ballad in a simple garb, and this task has undoubtedly been fulfilled with marked success.

The village bard of the present text is a muslim and almost all the characters are portrayed as holy warriors of ***'Din.'*** The under current that flows through the tale is mainly a sense of hatred against the Kaffir Ingrej. Hafis, the son of one Mugal, as it is narrated in the beginning of the story, requested his father to submit resignation from the service of the Police department of the British Government. To Hafis it was 'haram'—a great sin. He was ready to live by begging but could never surrender to the notorious Ingrej.

Rabai Patni, the fisher man, adopted Islam at his will, for security and prestige. Virtuous muslims of different places helped the fugitives by offering food and shelter. The selfish, autocrat and anti-nationals betrayed their cause and helped the Government in many ways. But against all odds and sufferings the warriors retained their undaunted spirit of sacrifice and dedication to their commitment. They embraced the glorious death of martyrs. They performed the funeral ceremonies with great honour and sanctity and never failed to observe rituals even in the crucial juncture of life and death. All these activities of the great warriors and their ideological and psychological attitudes are the reflections of the socio-religious and political trend of the people of the region, particularly muslims, in a greater extent.

The Sannyasi-Fakir rebellion [1763], Revolt of Nawab Radharam [1786], insurrection of Aga Muhammad Reza [1793], Faraizi movement of Saraiat ullah in Bengal [1804], the Wahabi Movement [1806-1873], Tarika I Muhammadi Movement of Sayed Ahmed Brelvi in Sylhet [1820-1821], Narkel beria Larai [Titu Mir, 1825-1831], Khilafat and Non Cooperation Movement Sylhet-Cachar [1920-1922], firing of the police in the annual meet of Kanaighat Madrasa [March 20, 1922], Chhinna Koraner mamla in Sylhet [April 8, 1922], Civil Disobedience Movement [1930-1932], Freedom Movement, rise of Muslim League and the Referendum of Sylhet to Pakistan — all these incidents and the political movements incited and inspired the majority section of the Muslim of the region Surma-Barak Valley, not only to rise against the British rule but also to settle down the question of self determination on the basis of religion.

It is evident that the immediate cause of the mutiny as it is narrated in the ballad is religion. Ramesh Chandra Majumdar admits that, "The other causes might be regarded as, more or less, contributory, in a rather remote sense, but the direct and the most important cause must have been the religious scruples to which the Hindus and the Muslims are peculiarly sensitive."[2] He also reviewed the character of the mutiny and pointed out that the contemporary Englishmen generally viewed upon the outbreak as a handiwork of the Muslims.[3] He also observed that, not only the Europeans, but even the Muslims themselves, at least a section of them, believed that they were the senior partners in the great undertaking.[4] To justify his views, he quoted Sir Syed Ahmed, an eminent leader of the Indian Muslims in the nineteenth century and who himself played an important role in the Mutiny, —"The Muslims were in every respect more dissatisfied than the Hindus, and hence in most districts they were comparatively more rebellious, though latter were not wanting in this respect".[5]

The part played by the Muslims was keenly experienced by many Englishmen and many of them expressed their opinions that the Muslims either deserted the British or joined with the rebels.[6] C. Raikes, even did not hesitate to remark that, "a Mohammedan was another word for a rebel".[7] Raikes also stated that, "They (the Muslims) have behaved in the part of India where I had jurisdiction, very ill; so ill indeed that if the rest of the population had sympathized with them, instead of antagonized, I should despair of governing India for future".[8] Roberts, who became a Field Marshal later on, angrily expressed that, "he would show these rascally Musalmans that, with God's help, Englishmen will still be master of India.[9] Coopland observed that the upheaval was their own doing and the Muslims are themselves to be blamed for carnage.[10] "They (Muslims), were the most blood thirsty, when the Mutiny did breakout", said Captain P.C. Scot.[11] Some historians of our country are also of the opinion that the Muslims played an important role than the Hindus. And that there was firm determination and intention among the leaders, and even among the Muslim community in general, to recapture the power from the British. Several proclamation. and pamphlets which were announced and distributed at the time of uprise in the different parts of the country clearly indicate their attitude.

The Muslim Chiefs in Avadh and Rohilakhand made an

appeal to the Muslims in the name of their religion, and remind them in their faith in the holy *Quran,* that by fighting against the infidels or paying money to others to fight, they would secure to themselves eternal beatitude. To the Hindus also the appeal was made in the name of their religion by pointing out how the British Government defiled it by introducing the re-marriage of widows, the abolition of 'Sati' etc. To the native rulers also, referring to the annexation of states, appeal was made in the name of religion. The proclamation announced a such, "Be it known to all of you that if these English are permitted to remain in India they will butcher you all and put an end to your religion".[12]

Bargie Qadr of Avadh and Liaqat Ali of Allahabad, all urging the Muslims to rise against the British in the name of religion. The proclamation begins with a quotation from *Quran* and concludes that, the friendship with Christians is heresy and hence it is a duty of all the Muslims to make themselves inveterate foes of these Christians. It contains throughout the proclamation,, the exhortation to the Muslim to rise against the English and extirpate them by holding out the dire consequences that would follow to the Muslim if the English got victory.[13]

A series of letters written and widely distributed by Mr. Edward, confirm the activities of the Christian Missionaries beyond doubt. In the letters, wherein it was expressed nakedly that, "as all India obeyed one Government, as all party of the country kept to constant communication one with the other by means of the electric, telegraph, and as the railway system united the different extremes of these great peninsula, it was necessary that there should be but one religion also, and proper, therefore, that every one should embrace Christianity".[14] Even it was threatened that all classes of natives, if required, are to be converted by force. The men of the 34th Native Infantry with whom the whole of the trouble began, were almost convinced that they would be converted to Christianity in any opportune moment.

Surendra Nath Sen observes, that "the outraged people identified the Christian Missionaries with the Christian Government because the Missionary was sometimes attended by the police. He quotes from Syed Ahmed in support of his views, where Ahmed states, "It has been commonly believed that Government appointed Missionaries and maintained them at its own cost".[15] Sen further opines that, "while the Hindus and Muslims gave discourses on their respective creeds at their private residences, temples or mosques, the Missionaries went to public places to denounce other people's creeds to the most violent terms".[16] Taken into account the reaction of both the Hindus and Muslims, Sen remarks, "The enlightened in his tolerant attitude might concede that ultimately all religions led to God, but the Muslims who firmly believed that his was the only true faith could not logically make that concession. The Muslim did not consider himself morally responsible for any heresy or lapse on the part of his progeny".[17]

Besides all these opinion, it is evident that both the Hindus and the Muslims equally broke into the war against the British Raj in 1857. Hiren Mukherjee rightly opines that the "Indian revolt of 1857, was the country's desperate bid for freedom. It brought together all alliance of more diverse forces than had ever united in India against a foreign conqueror. This alliance had to be put down with implacable violence before British power could recover itself".[18] He also observes that, "In its nature, it was a massive and often ferocious upheaval against not only the political supremacy of

British but also against the whole new order of things she had been importing into India. It was infinitely more than a military and even mainly Muslim insurrection which, on certain kinds of evidences, it might appear to be".[19]

The prime object of the struggle was to expel the infidels, the end of the alien foreign rule and regain the national sovereignty. Thomas Lowe in his contemporary account, 'Central India During the Rebellion', described the situation as such, 'Ruin, ruin, poverty,... had touched the land,... no one has the eyes and ears to use, can doubt for a moment that we have almost totally neglected the resources of such a mighty country, while we have introduced the trash of our manufacturing towns into very cranny of the land. We had endeavoured to destroy every inherent useful production by Western merchandise'.[20] He also quoted a distressed villager's statement that 'the jungles, the trees, the rivers, the wells, all the villages, and all the holy cities belong to the Sirkar. They have taken all,—everything. Very good, but what can we do?'[21] These painful words of a villager to Thomas Lowe was not only the words of an individual but of the desperate nation. Such situations compelled the mass to participate in the popular insurrection. The ballad,'Jangiyar Geet' and other songs of the Mutiny 1857 of the North-Eastern part of the country, especially the valley of Surma-Barak; and the notable collections of folk songs by Puran Chand Joshi from different parts of the country like Meerut, Aligarh, Oudh, Lucknow, Jhansi, Danapur etc. related to the great episodes of the glorious struggle of 1857,[22] all these undoubtedly establish the fact that the psychological and ideological attitude and the political aspirations of the Indian mass during the Mutiny period of 1857 was one and unique.

The Wahabis also fought heroically against the British

with a firm conviction to expel the infidels from the country in order to establish Dar- Ul- Islam, that is, the kingdom of Islam. "The political 'Jihads' of the Wahabis", remarks Hiren Mukherjee, "emphasized the role of the Muslim community of India as a religio-political unit. This was to happen again in the time of the 'Mutiny' of 1857 and the post-mutiny' phase of the Wahabis movements'.[23]

Q. Ahmed opines that, "The prevailing socio-religious degradation and the increasing loss of political powers to the non- Muslims were the two forces behind the rise of the movement. The two essential features of the movement, in fact were the amelioration of the society as well as the winning back of the 'country', freedom from the 'European infidels'. For the achievement of one, it was necessary to abstain from 'pernicious religious innovation' and for the other to resort to Zihad whose virtues and advantages have been repeatedly extolled".[24]

It is curiously observed by the historians that Wahabis were the most violent anti-British militant organization as a body and kept them aloof from the eventful days of the Mutiny. The practical reason behind such activities of the Wahabis was, as Ramesh Ch. Majumdar observes, "that the Wahabis favoured a purely Islamic movement and did not like to co-operate with the Hindus".[25] The Wahabis who joined the mutineers at Delhi they printed and published a proclamation, wherein they invited all Muslims to lift their arms for their religion. They declared that it was the duty of the Muslims to participates in the religious war against the English".[26]

The Wahabis role against the British prior to 1857, in Bengal and Bihar, successfully tried to unite the Muslims and a sense of hatred developed throughout the region. The circular which addressed to all the districts of Bengal and Bihar urging the Muslims to proceed to Mulk-a sittana in order to carry on a Jihad against the British deeply impressed the whole community. R.C. Majumdar also observes that, "The Muslims in the different parts of Bengal raised their arms in the name of Islam against the British and often against the Hindus too. The Wahabi sect created disturbances in Bengal under the leadership of Titumir who committed violent outrage on the life, faith and property of the Hindus. He proclaimed the extinction of the British Government and claimed, 'the sovereign power as the hereditary right of the Muslims which had been unjustly usurped by the Europeans.' The Wahabis established their influence in three districts in Bengal routed a contingent of Calcutta militia. Later, a well-equipped military force was sent against them. Titu fought a pitched battle and was killed in 1831."[27]

It is interesting to note that, the highest religious authoriuty of Islam, of the holy Makkah, was requested to give their opinion on the question whether British ruled country India can be treated as Dar-ul-Islam or not. The questions and the answers of these were as follows:

DECISION OF THE MAKKAH LAW DOCTORS

(The Heads of the Three Great Musalman Sects)

"Question:

'What is your opinion (May your greatness continue for ever) on the question: whether the country of Hindustan, the rulers of which are Christians, and who do not interfere with all the injunctions of Islam such as the ordinary daily Prayers, the Prayers of the two 'Ids, etc., but do authorize departure from a few of the injunctions of Islam, such as the permission to inherit the property of the Muhammadan ancestor to one who changes his religion (being that of his ancestors) and becomes a Christian, is Dar-ul-Islam or not? Answer the above, for which God will reward you'.

Answer No. 1:

'All praises are due to the Almighty Who is the Lord of all the Creation, Oh, Almighty, increase my knowledge.

As long as even some of the peculiar observances of Islam prevail in it, it is Dar-ul-Islam.

The Almighty is Omniscient, Pure and High:

This is the Order passed by one who hopes for the secret favour of the Almighty, who praises God, and prays for blessings and peace on his Prophet.

(Signed). *JAMAL IBN ABDULLAH SHEIKH OMARUL HANAFI,* the present Mufti of Makkah (the Honoured). May God favour him and his father'.

Answer II:

'All praises are due to God, Who is one; and may the blessings of God be showered upon our Chief, Muhammad, and upon his descendants and companions and upon the followers of his faith.

Oh God! I require guidance from Thee in righteousness.

Yes! As long as even some of the peculiar observances of Islam prevail in it, it is Dar-ul-Islam.

The Almighty is Omniscient, Pure and High.

This is written by one who hopes for salvation from the God of mercy. May God forgive him, and his parents, and preceptors and brothers and friends and all Muhammadans.

(Signed). *AHMAD IBN ZAINI DAHLAN,* Mufti of the Shafi sect of Makkah (the Protected) '

Answer III:

'All praises are due to God, who is one! O! Almighty! Increase my knowledge.

It is written the commentary of Dasoki that a Country of Islam does not become Dar-ul-Harb as soon as it passes into the hands of the infidels, but only when all or most of the injunctions of Islam disappear therefrom.

God is omniscent! may the blessings of God be showered upon our Chief, Muhammad, and on his decendants and companions.

(Signed.) Written by: *HOSSAIN-BIN-IBRAHIM,* Mufti of the Maliki sect of Makkah (the Illustrious)".

THE DECISION OF THE LAW DOCTORS OF NORTHERN INDIA

TRANSALATION OF THE ISTIFA OR QUESTION, PUT BY *SAYYID AMIR HUSSAIN,* PERSONAL ASSISTANT TO THE COMMISSIONER OF BHAGALPUR.

What is your decision, O men of learning and expounders of the law of Islam, in the following? –

Whether a Jihad is lawful in India, a country formely held by a Muhammadan ruler and now held under the sway of Christian Government, where the said Christian ruler does in no way interfere with his Muhammadan subjects in the Rites prescribed by their Religion, such as Praying, Fasting,

Pilgrimage, Zakat, Friday Prayer, and Zama'at, and gives them fullest protection and liberty in the above respects in the same way as a Muhammadan ruler would do, and where the Muhammadan subjects have no strength and means to fight with their rulers: on the contrary there is every chance of the war, if waged, ending with a defeat, and thereby causing an indignity to Islam.

Please answer, quoting your authority.

Fatwa dated the 17th Rabi-us-sani 1287 H., corresponding with the 17th July, 1870:

The Musalmans here are protected by Christians, and there is no Jihad in a country where protection is afforded, as the absence of protection and liberty between Musalmans and Infidels is essential in a religious war, and that condition does not exist here. Besides, it is necessary that there should be a probability of victory to Musalman and glory to Islam. If there be no such probability, the Jihad is unlawful.

Here the Maulavis quote Arabic passages from Manhaj-ul- Ghaffar and Fatawai- I -Alamgiri; supporting the decision.

MAULAVI ALI MUHAMMAD, of Lucknow;
MAULAVI ABDUL HAI, of Lucknow;
MAULAVI FAZIULLAH, of Lucknow;
MAULAVI MUHAMMAD NAIM, of Lucknow;
MAULAVI RAHAMATULLAH, of Lucknow;
MAULAVI KUTAB-UD-DIN, of Delhi
MAULAVI LUTFULLAH, of Rampur; and others.

DECISION OF THE CALCUTTA MUHAMMADAN SOCIETY

After declaring, in opposition to the Northern Law Doctors, that India is a Dar-ul-Islam, *Maulavi Karamat Ali* proceeded thus:

"The second question is, 'whether it is lawful in this country to make Jihad or not.' This has been solved together with the first. For Jihad can by no means be lawfully made in Dar-ul-Islam. This is no evident that it requires no argument or authority to support it. Now, if any misguided wretch, owing to pervers fortune, were to wage war against the Ruling powers of this country, British India; such war would be rightly pronounced rebellion; and rebellion is strictly forbidden by the Muhammadan law. Therefore such war, will likewise be unlawful; and in case any one would wage such war, the Muahammadan subjects would be bound to assist their Rulers, and in conjuction with their Rulers, to fight with such rebels. The above has been clearly laid down in the Fatawai-I-Alamgiri".[28]

Sannyasi-Fakir rebellion and Faraizi movement also had a prominent role in the history of the movements against the British. Almost at the very beginning of the British rule, the foreign power had to face the uprise of the Sannyasi and Fakirs in Bengal. After the Great Famine of 1770, the activities of Sannyasis and the Fakirs threatened to sweep away the English power. 'Faraizi' sect founded by Sariat Ullah (Sharkat-Ullah) in Bengal for religious reform, began to preach his doctrine in Dacca in 1824. Gradually the movement turned into a political one and he declared the country under British as a Dar-ul-harb, the country where the true Musalman should not live'.[29]

The root of the word Faraizi is Arabic *Farizah*, in plural *Faraiz*. They admit the obligation of only the first two of the five Muhammedan duties *Farz* and *Wajib*. The doctrine of the beliefs is that the rejection of *Farz* makes a man infidel and the rejection of *Wajib* makes a man an sinful Musalman. They rejected all non-essential parts of Islam and declared themselves as 'New Musalman'. In 1831 they fought with Calcutta Militia beat back the detachment. Gradually they became popular and a threat to the British authority. About eighty thousand followers under the leadership of Shariat-Ullah spread over the every district of Bengal raised jihad against the infidels. Maulavi Yahya Ali, the Chief Priest and Khalif of Wahabis of Patna amalgamated the Faraizis of Lower Bengal with the Wahabis of Northern India: Describing the role of Yahya Ali, Hunter states, " He corresponded with all the itinerant preachers as Spiritual Director of the sect in India. He organized and personally worked a complicated system of drafts in a secret language, by which large sums were safely transmitted from the center of the Empire to the Rebel Camp beyond the Frontier. He conducted the public ministrations in the Mosque. He examined and passed the rifles for the Fanatic Host, delivered a course of divinity lectures to the students, and by private study acquired an intimate acquaintance with the Arabic Fathers. But the most delicate operation of the conspirators was the transmission of recruits from the Patna Propaganda, or Little Warehouse, as it was called in their secret language, to the Great warehouse or Rebel Camp beyond the Frontier. The Bengali convert was liable to a hundred awkward questions *en route*. [30]

It is interesting to note that in narrating the conspiracy of the Wahabis, Hunter pointed out, a sort of secret language in which the rebels used to pass their messages throughout the country. He had cited a few examples in his book as such: "A battle is called a lawsuit; God, the Law agent; Gold Muhars are called large red rubies, large Delhi gold-embroidered shoes, or large red birds; remittances on Gold Muhars are spoken of as rosaries of red beads, and remittances in money as the price of books and merchandise; drafts or money orders are called white stones, the amount being intimated by the number of white beads as on a rosary. – Official Papers."[31]

All these religio-political aspects, which are treated as a most potent cause of the mutiny, are also viewed as the primary cause of the rebellion in the folk ballad 'Jangiyar Geet'. In the beginning of the tale told by the village bard we have observed the attitude of Hafiz towards the English learning, and the service of his father in the government and his conviction to Islam, all these reaffirm the attitude of the mutineers of 1857. The savage act of the sahib provoked the excited soldiers to turn into rebellion. In the behaviour of the English man the general trend of the British officials of that days has been appropriately reflected. Condemning the behaviour of the English men towards the Indians, Syed Ahmed rightly said, 'Their pride and arrogance led them to consider the natives of India as undeserving the name of human beings'. He also noticed that such ill-treatment was, 'more offensive to Muslims who for centuries past have received special honour and enjoyed immunities in Hindustan."[32]

The heroic-tale narrates that when the fugitives arrived at *Kuia Khalar par*, there they met one fisherman named as *Rabai Patni*. Rabai offered them food and shelter. He also managed to divert the English force in a wrong direction and saved the rebellious force from dire consequences. The ideas and the virtuous spirit, the amicable nature and the dedication of the holy warriors, impressed and inspired Rabai to embrace Islam. The Jangis then rushed towards Langla. Before marching they left two persons with Rabai for educating them in Islamic education. The incident of Rabai Patni, a Hindu fisherman, who was converted into Islam, is an interesting study in the religio-social and political movement of the Mahimals, i.e., the Muslim fisherman community, of this region. Before the advent of Islam in the region, a bulk of population of this region had been fishermen by profession. They were looked down upon by the caste Hindus and regarded as untouchables and outcastes.

Hunter dealt the matter of conversion to Islam in the Southern part of Bengal particularly the south of Dacca and Bikrampur and ascertained after personal enquiries in the district of Faridpur, Bhakharganj and the Sundarban areas, he was of the opinion that, "The greater part of the peasant population throughout Eastern Bengal is Muhammadan. In those districts of overwhelming rivers and boundless swamps, the aborigines were never admitted into the respectable Hindu community. The Aryan migration southwards had not penetrated in sufficient strength into the sea board and Deltaic tracts, to thoroughly pound down in the Brahmanical mortar the earlier people of the soil. They accordingly remained beyond the pale of Hinduism, outcastes fishing in their remote estuaries, and reaping hazardous rice crops from their flooded lands, without social status or religious rites. So impure are they, that a Brahman of the highest caste cannot settle among them without taint, and in a few generations his descendants cease to have *jus connubii* with the Brahman community a few days' journey to the north, from which they sprang. The Muhammadans recognized no such distinctions. They came down upon the country, sometimes as military colonists, sometimes as heads of great reclamation enterprises in the Deltaic Districts. Even in an old settled District like Jessore, the earlier traditions begin with an enterprise of the latter sort. As the primeval heroes of the inner parts of India slew monster beasts, quelled demon tribes, and hewed down the all-covering forest; so the first object that looms on the pre–historic horizon in Deltaic tracts is the man who pushed forward tillage into the regions formerly the prey of the sea. The Mussalmans led several of these great land reclamation colonies to the southward, and have left their names in Eastern Bengal as the first dividers of the water from the land. The sportsman comes across their dykes, and matalled roads, and mosques, and tanks, and tombs, in the loneliest recesses of the jungle; and wherever they went, they spread their faith, partly by the sword, but chiefly by a bold appeal to the two great instincts of the popular heart. The Hindus had never admitted the amphibious population of the delta within the pale of their community. The Muhammadans offered the plenary privileges of Islam to Brahman and outcaste alike: 'Down on your knees, everyone of you', preached these fierce missionaries, 'before the Almighty, in whose sight all men are equal, all created beings as the dust of the earth. There is no God but the one God, and His messenger is Muhammad.' The battle-cry of the warrior became, as soon as the conquest was over, the text of the divine."[33]

History and the folk traditions of this region also confirm the fact that when Hazrat Sahjalal invaded Sylhet in 1328, a large scale conversion was followed, due to the efforts of 360 numbers of Aulias.[34] The oppressed and downtrodden amongst the Hindus felt inspired by the egalitarian philosophy of the new religion. A bulk of the fisherman community and peasantry embraced Islam in the wake of the new socio-political movements in the hope that the new faith would provide them with social justice. Raj Mohan Nath opines that "The process (of conversion to Islam) started in 1304, and within a very short time, due to the efforts of 360 followers of Shahjalal, they increased their number, being indirectly helped by the Hindus who preferred to be outnumbered, blindly sticking to the policy of weakening their race by elimination. The so-called low castes formed the majority of the converts."[35]

Rabai's urge for Islamic education and the cordial respond of the Jangis in view of establishing a Madrasa in the village, this incident bears a conformity with the aspiration and attitude of the Muslims of the region for religious education.

We have learnt from the history, that in the beginning of the seventeenth century, Moulana Zia Uddin of Sylhet established a Madrasa in the town. The Mughal Emperor donated Lakheraj-land to one Mufti Asim for that noble purpose. Both the Hindus and Muslims were educated in Arabic and Persian in that Institution as Persian was the language of the Court for centuries in the Shahi Amal. From the book *'Foster's Memoirs'*, it is also learnt that the Madrasa was in existence in the year 1827.[36]

One of the most important feature of the *Ballad* is that it contains about 138 numbers of Perso- Arabic words. The reason behind such an influence is religio-ethnic. The district of Karimganj from where the present text has been collected and within the areas where the popularity of the songs belong, is mainly dominated by the Muslims. The village bard himself belongs to that community. The Muslims of the region like other parts of Bengal adopted these foreign elements owing to religio-political and cultural causes. It may be mentioned here that the district of Sylhet was transferred to Assam in the year 1874 and before that this part was a part and percel of Bengal since Turk-Afgan period.

From the period of Hussin Shah, since 16th Century A.D., the Islamic education and culture in Sylhet and other parts of Bengal were flourishing. The Muslims of Sylhet were in direct contact with the Muslims of the Northwest provinces of India for centuries.[37] As a result the North-Western Islamic culture and language influenced Surma-Barak like other parts of Bengal. Narrating the socio-cultural and linguistic characteristics of the region Acharyya Suniti Kumar Chatterji remarks that, "Hindustan made itself the inheritor and propagator of the Persian and Moslim spirit in India, from the 17th and 18th Century; and it came to Bengal and Persian words, which formerly were brought into Bengali most directly, now began to be admitted in larger numbers through Hindostani in to Bengali and the various other vernaculars of the land. The result of it all was that towards the end of the 18th Century, the Bengali speech of the upper classes, even among Hindus, was highly Persianised."[38] He also pointed out that "Many of the practices of the Sultan's darbar at Gaur were adopted by the petty chiefs of Bengal, and engrafted on the old Hindu court customs and etiquettes which were preserved in the independent states of Orissa (Jajnagar), Vishnupur, Tirhut, Tippera, Sylhet and Kamrupa. This meant an addition of Persian terms to the vocabulary of the Bengali. The Moslem Kasi (Qudi) or district officer, who had control over the general administration, the Amin or governor and in later times the Faujdar or military magistrate as well as the revenue officials, brought to the people of Bengal Persian words connected with justice, revenue and general administration: and the number of such words even now in use in Bengali in quite a large one."[39]

But in 1836 the introduction of English replaced Persian as a Court language and subsequently the said Madrasa was closed down. Such an act of the government obviously wounded the sentiment of the Muslims.

In Sylhet the first English School was established in the year 1840-41. Subsequently it was upgraded in to a Zilla School in pursuance of the new policy on education laid down in 'Woods Despatch', 1854.[40] The Muslims did not accept this policy of the British heartily, rather the entire affairs were looked upon as a conspiracy against their religious faith. The enrolment of the Muslim students was so poor than Hindus in the aforesaid English School in Sylhet, that the School Committee reviewed the matter seriously and suggested to introduce Arabic and Persian to encourage the Muslims to share with the new education policy. But the general committee of Public Instructions turned down the proposal. Renowned historian Syed Murtaza Ali of Bangladesh, quotes a report in his book from *'The British Policy and the Muslims of Bengal'*. This report clearly shows the apathy of the Muslims to the new education policy. The following data of enrolment, as it is shown in the table clearly reveals the trend of the people of that period:[41]

Years	*Hindus*	*Muslims*
1841	73	02
1846	42	02
1852	60	11
1856	157	05

However, this school was abolished during the dark days of the mutiny and for some little time Sylhet was without any English School. After the Mutiny, Reverend William Pryse, a Missionary of the Presbyterian Mission, established another School in Sylhet. This Missionary was renowned as the father of English education in the valley.[42]

In the district of Cachar the first government English High School was established at Silcher in December, 1863. The Muslims of the Valley, in those days, were also quite indifferent with the New education policy. A report of the Inspector of the Schools on Public Instructions of Assam, in 1877-78, reviewed the matter as such. "It would appear that Musalmans as a rule are not connected with a mere secular education, and indeed, to a great extent are indifferent to secular education at all. They will go in large number to Maktabs where the Quoran is taught by rot. There can be be little doubt, but in that educational matters, Mohammedans generally display an amount of apathy which is not to be found in their Hindu brethrens."[43]

In 1826, Scott tried for the promotion of indigenous education in Assam. Accordingly the Government of Bengal decided to establish a number of Schools there. The subjects mainly taught in these Schools were Sanscrit, Shastras and in some Schools elementary knowledge of arithmetic, medicine and astronomy were in the curriculum. In 1831, another school was established at Gauhati by Capt. White in collaboration with a Christian Missionary James Rae. In this Institution translated version in Bengali from English book on elementary science was introduced.

It is also learnt from the Report of Public Instruction Bengal that, "a number of indigenous schools were started in some districts entirely at public expense, and that to encourage such institutions, on the advice of the local educational authorities, the Government of Bengal had introduced, in the same year, the subsidy system, under which a grant of Re.1 p.m. was made for every ten boys under instruction. In

1857-58, the number of pupils receiving instruction in such schools was 750 in Sibsagar and 600 in Kamrup.[44]

In 1857-58 the number of village schools was 78 with a total enrolment was about three thousand. In a few indigenous schools sponsored by the public the teachers were mostly Assamese of both Hindus and Muslims. The medium of Instruction was Bengali. It is observed that in the government schools at Sibsagar and Gauhati Urdu and Persian were also taught under private arrangement.

In Sylhet and Cachar the Muslims carried out religious education by establishing Mufti Schools, Maktabs and Madrassas to educate themselves in Islam. Of course, it is evident that such intentions were also prevailed throughout the country in those days. Actually the policy of education of the British Government and the absense of efficient system of education for all classes of Muslims also made them apathetic in this regard. "The Bengal Musalmans," Hunter rightly observed, "can never hope to succeed in life, or to obtain a fair share of the State patronage, until they fit themselves for it, and they will never thus fit themselves until provision is made for their education in our schools.... The English in India have failed in their duty towards the Musalmans; but it is only fair to narrate the difficulties and discouragements which they have met with in endeavouring do it."[45]

From more than half a century Muslims in Bengal particularly in Eastern and lower parts of the region were neglected and deprived of Education. They were excluded even from the more active career opportunities of their life. Narrating the situation Hunter stated, "In 1781 the Governor General discerned the change which must inevitably come over the prospects of the Musalmans, and tried to prepare them for it. As the wealth of the great Muhammadan Houses decayed, their power of giving their sons an education which should fit them for the higher offices in the State declined *pari passu*. To restore the chances in their favour, Warren Hastings established a Muhammadan College in the Capital, and 'endowed it with certain rents towards its perpetual maintenance'. Unfortunately for the Musalmans, he left its management to the Musalmans themselves. Persian and Arabic remained the sole subjects of instruction, long after Persian and Arabic had ceased to be the bread-winners in official life. Abuse of very grave character crept into the College and in 1819 it was found necessary to appoint a European Secretary. On 1826 a further effort was made to adapt the Institution to the altered necessities of the times; an English class was formed, but unhappily soon afterwards broken up. During the next quarter of a century, the Muhammadan College shared the fate of the Muhammadan community."[46]

Again between the year 1851-1853, the College was reorganized into two departments. The Upper class was purely for Arabic studies and lower class for Anglo-Persian. But all these efforts ultimately failed to solve the problems rather, "The whole system, says the most distinguished Musalman reformer of the day, Maulavi Abd-ul -Latif Khan Bahadur, can land them only in half-and-half results. As a students entirely of Arabic, they lose the benefit of the little English training they were acquainted with; for the college has no means for continuing English instructions, and it does not take much time to obliterate from their minds whatever little English they may have learned."[47]

The statistics which W.W. Hunter provided in his book clearly indicate the pathetic place of the Muslims in the Civil Services, in 1871. It is found that in that period the State in the Department of Public Instruction only one Muslim was capable of holding the position out of 53.[48]

However, it is evident that the Muslims in general were indifferent and gradually became hostile with the British Raj. Those who owed allegiance, they submitted to the power for personal, political or other vested interests. The role of the Local Zamindars, affluents and other vested interested middle class, traders both the Hindus and Muslims were admired by the Supreme authority. It is observed that after the proclamation of Palmarston in the British Parliament in the discussion the authority expressed their expectation in this way that, " We therefore hope that the Rajahs of Bengal and other wealthy men will establish and support undertaking of promise."[49]

Ratan Lal Chakrabarty in his account mentioned the names of a few loyal Zamindars who with their all efforts served the Company in 1857 like, — Abdul Gani of Dacca, Kalinarayan Roychoudhury of Bhawal pargana, Kalindi Rani of Chittagong, Rajah Baroda Kanta Roy of Jessore, Rani Swarnamoyee of Rangpur, Bijoy Gobinda Choudhury of Pabna and Syed Amir Ali, Gauranga Chandra Roy, Khuda Bax Shah, Khedmat Shah Fakir, Iyasin Shah Fakir etc.[50]

The Zamindar of Pabna, Radha Gobindo Choudhury owed his allegiance to the British authority and submitted in the words that, "Your petitioner feels that it is the duty of every loyal subjects to assist the government during this state of things and though the Government is strong enough to check them out of the resources already at its disposal, yet your petitioner has been during these days contemplating of some means of opposing them, should they ever chance to come this way to Pabna."[51]

The Zamindar of Choudhury family of Pratapgarh Pargana, Kala Mia of Latu, Suruj Mia of Biskut of the district of Sylhet belonged to the same class whom the mass had treated as traitors. There were persons in this region Surma-Barak, like other parts of the country, who harvested their fortunes in opportune moments rendering adequate and sincere service to the British. It is evidently a fact, that "The new westernized and English educated section was on the British side. Its leaders condemned the rising in unequivocal terms. The educated Indian citizens of Calcutta and the landed aristocrats and feudals of Bengal and Madras were loud in their denunciation of the mutiny and the mutineers. The rising of the 'so-called' Bengal army, however aroused no sympathy from the educated people in Bengal. On the other hand they were eager to demonstrate their loyalty to the Raj which suddenly seemed to be on trial. It is observed that, on May 22, 1857, the committee of the British Indian Association at a special meeting passed resolutions condemning, 'the disgraceful and mutinous conduct of the native solidarity', and protesting against the reports about popular sympathy for the mutinéers. The resolutions were forwarded to Lord Canning with a covering letter by Raja Radha Kanta Deb and others. These were also circulated among the people of the mufasil, so that they might not lose faith in the power and good intentions of the Government. The Calcutta Traders Association, the French and the Armanian citizens of Calcutta, some Indian communities in the city and the suburbs separately addressed the Governor General on the question, many of them offering their personal services. The Hindu Patriot, expressed its conviction that the British Government in India would soon get over the difficulty.[52]

The British Indian Association took a leading part in the loyalty demonstration organized in Calcutta on May 24, 1857, under the Chairmanship of Kali Krishna Deb of Sobha Bazar. The radical section was represented by Ramgopal Ghosh, Girish Chandra Ghosh and Kashi Prasad Ghosh, as was the Landed aristocracy by Ramanath Tagore, Digambar Mitra and Jay Krishna Mukherjee of Uttarpara. "It was decided in the meeting that the proceedings would be translated in to the regional languages and distributed in a printed form for mass circulation".[53]

It is interesting to note that, "Every one present in the meeting seemed to fall over himself to display the loyalty."[54]

Many of them wished to be enlisted as special constables and to serve with the Europeans. Several big landed proprietors demanded that the Government should allow them to arm their retainers on its behalf. Finally, they assured the Government of their solid support and submit the loyalty of the Bengal peasantry. The leading Newspaper, *'The Bengal Harkara'*, welcomed these 'protestations of loyalty'.[55] It is also further observed that the Divisional Commissioner of Burdwan was pleased with the Maharaja of Burdwan who rendered every assistance to the Magistrate for the transport of European troops.

On June 18, 1857, the Zamindars, Talukdars and other inhabitants of Uttarpara and its neighborhood headed by Jay Krishna, sent a petition to the Magistrate of Hoogly, drawing attention to the problems centering the mutiny and offered some practical suggestions. The petitioners began by thanking the Government for the measures the authority had adopted to suppress the revolt. The disarming of the sepoys of the Presidency Division had greatly relieved their fears. But the disbanded sepoys, the dissectors who for obvious reasons were unable to go home posed a problem to the district. They would linger in Bengal and be without any means of livelihood; and they would be a constant source of danger. They apprehended that, "the zamindars' retainers, with their father, son, or brothers among the rebels, might desert and join the sepoys when the time for action would come. At this juncture it would be unwise to rely on them. All these, said the petitioners, rendered the life and property of the people unsafe."[56]

All these so called 'bhadra lok' feudals, landlords and other 'golams' of the British power whom the people regarded as their leader, forgetting their ideological differences, shamelessly cooperated with the government in every possible way. Prasanna Kumar Tagore, Ramgopal Ghosh and Rama Prasad Roy served on the general committee which organized a fund for the relief of the sufferers who began arriving in Calcutta from the disturbed districts. Some shrewd Baniyas and mutsuddis, who had no doubt about the final success of the East India Company, profited by the prevailing opportune moment. It is also noticed that, "when many the British were on their way out, a few wealthy persons like Rani Rasmani are known have brought up enormous quantities of the Company's stock at rock bottom prices. They had a good time during the Imperial heyday which followed the mutiny."[57]

Rajnarayan Basu, the 'grandfather of Indian Nationalism', illustrated how the educated Bengali people avoided the mutiny like plague. In 1857, Rajnarayan was the Headmaster of the Zilla School of Midnapore. During the period of panic he and his colleagues attended the School wearing dhoti underneath their trousers so that they could appear before the rebel sepoys in their Indian dress. They had even carefully planned their routes of escape to avoid any sorts of chaos and confrontation. The peaceful sleep of Rajnarayan was also frequently disturbed by the frightening dreams in which he saw the sepoys in red uniforms.[58]

The *Hindu Patriot* of August 20, 1857, narrated about the attitude of the different section of the people and observed that,

"Peari Mohan Banerjee (1835-1874), an old student of Uttarpara Government School was working as Munsiff near Allahabad. When the mutiny broke out then a young man of 22, Peary Mohan, organized effective resistance to the mutineers. He displayed such courage and ability to plan operations as would have done credit to an army commander. For this he was called the 'Fighting Munsiff'. The Government of India recognized his services by giving him rewards and a Jaigir worth Rs.10,000/- in the district of Gorakh Pur."[59]

A very notable petition submitted by the loyal Elites, Zamindars, Citizens, servants and others addressed to the Governor-General of India which reveals the naked attitude of the aforesaid colonial slaves may be quoted here to judge the situation. It runs as follows:

"To

The Right Hon'ble *CHARLES JOHN VISCOUNT CANNING,*

Governor-General of India, &c. &c.

My Lord – we, the, undersigned Rajahs, Zamindars, Talukdars, Merchants, and other Natives of the province of Bengal, take the earliest opportunity, on the retaking of Delhi, to offer your Lordship in Council our warmest congratulations on the signal success which has attended the British arms, under circumstances unparallel in the annals of British India.

The establishment of British supremacy was considered to have been completely effected a century ago, when Clive led a few ill-trained battalions against the preponderating and well-equipped force which represented the Mogul power on the plains of Plassey. But whether the inadequacy of the means or the magnitude of that achievement, were more deserving of admiration, has not yet been determined by history. No difference of opinion, however, can exist, as to the recapture of Delhi, the details of which have recently been published for general information. Though no one capable of forming a judgment on the subject ever doubted for a moment of the speedy reduction of Delhi, yet some little misgiving might have been felt by those who know how well furnished was the place with the ammunitions of war, and occupied by what an immense number of men, whose fiendish animosity was excited to the utmost by that resolution, discipline, and acquaintance with the art of war, which they had acquired by long training in the ranks from which they had basely revolted. But there can be no question of the admiration with which the world will learn by what a handful of men the ardouse work has been achieved, in a brief period— with the with the limited resources, a most unlooked for exigency afforded, and amid discouragements arising from the unhealthiness of season, that were all but overwhelming.

We have derived sincere consolation from the reflection that in Bengal proper there has been no disturbance, not even a sumptom of disaffection; but that, on the contrary, the people have maintained that loyalty and devotion to the British Government, which led their ancestors to hail, and as far as they could to facilitate, the rising ascendancy of that power.

Under the fostering influence of that Government, the

population of the country has increased, its agriculture has extended, security has been to life and property and the value of land, both at the Presidency and in the interior, has been very considerably enhanced.

Sensible of the benefits they have enjoyed under British administration, the people could not but cordially sympatheise with the embarrassing position in which their rulers had suddenly been placed, and sincerely long for the speedy and entire re-establishment of British supremacy in the disturbed districts. So entirely have they identified their interests with those of their rulers, that the natives of Bengal, men, women, and children, have in every part of the scene of the mutinies, been exposed to the same rancour and treated with the same cruelty, which the mutineers and their misguided countrymen have displayed towards the British within their reach.

It has been a prominent object with your Lordship both effectually to crush the disaffected and rebellious, and to protect and re-assure the loyal and obedient. Accordingly, the extensive powers of legislation vested in your hands have been employed to punish crimes of every form and magnitude against the state with promptitude and rigour; to check vigorously the progress of sedition and disloyalty; and to give a guarantee to the people at large that those powers could be wielded with justice and discrimination, so as to guard as far as possible against faithful and innocent subjects being confounded with the disseminators of sedition and the perpetrators of open mutiny or secret treachery... permit us to hope that your Lordship in Council will receive our heartfelt congratulations on the eminent success which has crowned the British arms, and the warmest expressions of our confidence from the opportune display of those signal talents which have distinguished your administration in times of unexampled difficulty, and have largely contributed to the safety of the British empire in these region and the re-assurances of the peaceful and loyal.

We have the honor to be,

My·lord,

Your most obedient and faithful servants,

Sd. / *Maharajah Mahatab Chand Bahadoor, of Burdwan. Rajah Radhakant Bahadur, Rajah Kalikrishna Bahadur,* and others, inhabitants of Bengal, upwards of two thousand five hundred."[60]

The role of these loyal class was portrayed in the Calcutta Newspapers in a very adequate authenticity of that time. In Bengali it was reported that, 'both the Palaces of Shova bazaar are guarded by the armed sepoys. The Gora [European] Sipahis are roaring and marching, in numerous, in and around the house of Rani Rasmoni at Janbazar and the residences of Datta Babus' at Nalanda. The central area of the City from Kolu Tola to Bag Bazar, all the elite houses of the wealthy persons and the feudals like Sen, Shil, Dutta, Mullik, Tagore, Sinha, Ghosh, Mitra, Basu, Dev etc. are surrounded and protected by the Native sepoys and European Soldiers.'[61]

The attitude of these wealth-hungry and fortune- seekers was rightly reviewed and assessed by Gordon and remarked, "And from the last quarter of the eighteenth century, Calcutta was the arena in which those Bengalis who sought fame, fortune and solid accomplishment, had to climb the ropes of opportunity."[62]

In Dacca, in the Editorial column of *The Dacca News*, the

activities of 'The Hero of Dacca' Khaza Abdul Gani, was appreciated for his relentless service to the Government and the donation of Rs. 5 lakhs in the voluntary fund at the rate of five percent interest was also marked as a trust of loyalty towards the British Raj.[63]

It is also observed that Khaza Abdul Gani, "fortified his house and armed his family and retainers; at the same time to show his confidence in the British power, gave much valuable information to the authorities of the actual state of the country, and placed all his elephants, boats, horses, carriages etc. at their disposal."[64]

Abdul Gani clarifying his own position stated that, " My presence in the station at this critical moment inspires my countrymen with hope and confidence in the British Government and prevents the evil-doers from carrying out wicked designs. My absence, on the other hand, will cause a general panic precipitate matters which we are so anxious to prevent." [65]

In this region Surma-Barak we observe the same attitude shown by the loyal vested interested class. Achyut Charan Chodhury of Maina, Karimganj, did not hesitate, rather felt proud to announce that, his ancestors were very much loyal and helpful to the British in many crucial occasions like that of Nabab Radharam's rebellion (1786), Burmese war (1824), Kuki insurgency (1826-1872) and Sepoy mutiny (1857).[66] His ancestor not only deployed Kalamia against the mutineers but also personally wrote letters to Daroga of Latu and to the officiating superintendent Mr. R. Stewart, Silchar, district of Cachar. The superintendent acknowledging the fact writes in his dispatches, that "I have also received a letter from Choudhury of Juffirghur in Sylhet, apprising me of their having gone eastward with a view to cross over the hills in to my pergunnah of Serespore and Hylla Kandy".[67]

The Cachar Tea Company received fresh grant of lands for their services during the mutiny. Mr. Hogg and several others of the detachment received 'Indian Mutiny medal', cash awards and in several other ways.[68]

Learned historian Upendra Chandra Guha mentioned one Rai Hari Charan Sarma Bahadur and an extra assistant commissioner of this region who were honored with the Indian Medal.[69] Their high handedness often succeeded to seize or temper the documentary proof of their ancestos' loyal service. Mr. Jyotirmoy Sen, quoting from the Cachar district records cited a few instances and strikingly remarks, "A letter which bore the proof of that nasty incident (similar to that done by the Zamindar Kalamia) was found missing from the files of the Lushai Expedition and the disppearance of the document have saved the face of its doors".[70]

In Sylhet, the role of the Zamindars of Mazumdar family, in the Mutiny period was very much loyal. When the news of the advancement of the rebellious forces of 34th Native Infantry Regiment reached Sylhet the panic overshadowed the town. The Magistrate R.O. Heywood, being alarmed, had to sent his wife to Cherrapunji by the advice of the local Europeans.[71] Immediately after this incident, the shopkeepers shutted down their doors, the day labourers and boatsmen fled away leaving behind their jobs, the people abandoned the place and took their flight towards the remote villages.[72] In the meantime Zamindar Sayeed Bukht Majumdar set his cannons on the road sides before his houses to resist the rebels. Being alarmed at the situation the authority seized these artilleries. Later on to avoid humiliation the Zamindar transferred these cannons to the authority as presentation.[73]

It may be mentioned here that this Majumdar family was rewarded in various ways for rendering loyal services to the Government specially in the period of Lushai Expedition.[74]

In fact, other than these feudal landlords, the vested interested middle classes were also anxious for the continuance of the British Raj. *'The Dacca News'* published an elaborate article on this issue and expressed the Natives' feeling at that turmoil period of the Mutiny wherein it was remarked that, "The Zamindars are if possible still more anxious for the continuance of our Government. They are still with a very few exceptions, persons who have grown rich under our rule, and have invested their savings in the purchase of Zemindaries. Some of them are Bengali Omlah of the Mussulman zemindaries, and obtained possessions of the property of their masters, who hated nothing so much as business, and who never could understand accounts, but lending them money for their pleasures and debaucheries at high rate of interest and by employing the complicated machinery of our courts to complete their ruin, or even by using the more objectionable means of forgery for the same end. Such persons exist, merely because the strong government of the English enables them to do so."[75]

On the other hand, "Every where the heart of the Muslims of Bengal were in favour of the revolt. But it was a misfortune for the Muslims of Bengal, that they did not have good leaders. There was also a scarcity of resources—especially arms and ammunitions to carry on with the revolution." [76]

One of the most striking socio-religious feature of the

ballad 'Jangiyar geet' 'is the catholicity of its character. Here we should have to keep in mind the non-communal national character of the Great Mutiny. Though most of the characters are 'Mumin Musalmans' and they fought for a religious cause, and the village-bard is a devout follower of Islam, yet their heart is not debased by any narrow or illbred sentiments of racial prejudice. They took 'Zihad' against the animosity and political supremacy of the British. But against the counterpart Hindus, they never showed any sorts of rivalry or hatred. Rather the 'Geet' provides us with the fact that they were sympathetic and liberal. Not only in the present heroic- tale, but also in the whole of the folk literature of Bengal, the sense of secularism of the Muslim poets are highly prevailed. Particularly the Hymn portion of the folk- ballads or songs, as a rule, characterized by large hearted and sympathetic appreciation of each other's religious ideals.

The poet of *'Manjurma'* a popular folk-ballad puts it in the mouth of his hero that his wife was a fairy of Behest, a veritable flag of Heaven, sacred as a Tulsi leaf and beautiful as Daksha bhuja. The Mohamedan poet of the ballad *'Nurrunneha'* pays his salute to the Pirs and Saints as well as to the local Hindu deities – 'Baramai' and 'Srimai' in his prologue. Such a spirit of magnanimity of our rich tradition is also perfectly retained in the ballad 'Jangiyar Geet'. The Hymn recited in the preliminary portion of the 'Geet' is evidently a composition of Muslim minstrel and the sense of secularism of his views has been illustrated by the recognition of the Hindu shrines, God and goddesses, alongwith his own religious belief and wisdom. He pays his tributes by saying that, "I offer to the rising sun the benign Incarnation of light; - the light which removes all darkness at dawn. Oh Allah! the day is encircled by bad- omen. In the North, I offer my tribute to the Devas of Unakuti, who has assembled in a party. In the West, I pay my all honour to holy Macca and make my Salam to all the people of Hindusthan other than Hindus. In the South, I offer my tribute to the Kaliday Ocean; where a pelted stone takes six months to reach the bottom of it. Next I tender my all reverence to Allah and all Nabis. I salute my Murshid, all Aulias and all the people who have gathered here. Then, I bow down to the goddess Sarasvati for her blessings. Oh mother! it is you who have taken me in your shelter in my early boyhood of twelve years. Now in this old age of eighty, I hope you will not be unkind to me. If I am deprived from your blessings, you will be the killer of your sons Kartik and Ganesha. This way I pay homage to the all corners of the earth. Then I salute at first, Allah-Niranjan, Bibi, Ali, mother Fatemah, Hasan and Hussain. After that, I tender my salam to all Nabis and Ambiyas. And then I bow to the feet of my Murshid, my preceptor, parents and all Muslim brothers. Oh mother Jogini! now be gracious to come down and inspire me with songs. I offer my all reverence to you. God knows, what is written in the fate today, still this poor fellow is going to narrate the 'Geet'. Oh Allah! the day is encircled by the shadows of bad omen".[77]

Again in the narration of the incidents of Latu, while the arrested mutineers being tied by the chains in pairs were dragged by the British soldiers to the riverside for bathing, the popular scene of the emersion of the goddess 'Kali' instantly twinkled the vision of the Muslim poet. Again, Hindu Rabai Patni did not hesitate for a moment to come forward with the attitude of hospitality towards the Muslim warriors. The spirit of magnanimity of the village-bard of the folk-ballad invariably established the fact that, the society of that period of mutiny was free from the curse of communalism. All these incidents and their impact on the society, its religion and culture, definitely establish the truth that the unparallel outbreak of 1857 "produced conditions of war of Independence" and "a great and direct challenge to the British rule".[78]

And thus for obvious reasons this glorious struggle stirred the heart of the mass and their reaction and the response was unequivocally echoed in the songs and ballads. The folk of the vast land of the country experienced and witnessed, from Benaras to Allahabad, Jhansi to Arrah, Delhi to Dibrugarh and Latu to Binnakandi, the horrible cruelties of the British, by hanging enmasse, burning and devastating the houses, ruthless torturing on the insurgents and even on the innocents. The Folk-bards of the North and Central India composed innumerable songs, Rasos, Dohas and Panwars on the incidents related to the great rebellion,1857.[79] Likewise the bards of the North East, specially of Surma - Barak valley, also expressed their sentiments and reactions in songs and ballads with same tune and spirit.

All these attitudes, actionS and reactions of the common people reflected in their oral compositions, tell us the story of the other side of the history, — the history of our glorious past. It also help us to assess rightly the thought of the mass whose 'own talented sons were these unknown folk poets' and to look at the rebellion in a different light. Mackenzie was apparently right in his final statement where he honestly confessed that, 'Fate seems determine to prove that there shall be no rest for the English in India till they stand forth as Governors or advisorios of each tribe and people in land."[80] But it is also the fact that the lesson of patriotism and hatred of foreign domination ultimately led to the birth of Indian Nationalism.

NOTES

1. Quoted from *Jangiyar Geet*, lines 489-500.
2. Majumdar, Ramesh Chandra: *The Sepoy Mutiny and the Revolt of 1857*, Calcutta, 1957, p. 441.
3. *Ibid.*, p. 390.
4. *Ibid.*, p. 400.
5. *Ibid.*, p. 400.
6. *Ibid.*, p. 399.
7. *Ibid.*, p. 399, Quoted from Raikes. C. *Notes on the Revolt in the North-Eastern Province of India*, London.
8. *Ibid.*, p. 398.
9. *Ibid.*, p. 399.
10. *Ibid.*, p. 399.
11. *Ibid.*, p. 399.
12. *Ibid.*, p. 400.
13. *Ibid.*, p. 431.
14. *Ibid.*, p. 437.
15. Sen, Surendranath: *Eighteen Fifty Seven*,Government of India, New Delhi, 1958, p. 9.
16. *Ibid.*, p. 9.
17. *Ibid.*, p. 9.
18. Mukharjee, Hiren: *India's Struggle for Freedom*, Calcutta, 1968, p. 50.
19. *Ibid.*, p. 50.
20. Lowe, Charles Rath Bone: *Central India during the Rebellion*, pp. 357-58, quoted in Joshi, Puran Chand, *1857 in Folk Songs*, Introductory chapter, New Delhi, 1994, p. x.
21. *Ibid.*, pp. 358-59.
22. Joshi, Puran Chand: *1857 in Folk Songs* (compiled and edited), New Delhi, 1994.
23. Mukharjee, Hiren, *op.cit.*, p. 46.
24. Ahmed, Qeyamuddin: *The Wahabi Movement in India*, Calcutta, 1966, p. 15.
25. Majumdar, R.C., *ibid.*, p. 59.
26. *Ibid.*, p. 59.
27. *Ibid.*, pp. 59-60.

28. Hunter, W.W.: *The Indian Musalmans*, Dacca,1975, Appendix-I, II, III., pp. 197-200.
29. Majumdar, R.C., *op.cit.,* pp. 57-58.
30. Hunter, W.W., *op.cit.,* p. 29.
31. *Ibid.*, pp. 85.
32. Ahmed, Qayam Uddin, *op.cit.*, p. 26.
33. Hunter W.W., *op.cit.*, pp. 137-38.
34. The Aulias, see *Appendix.- E.*
35. Nath, Raj Mohan: *The Background of Assamese Culture,* Shillong, 1986, p. 122.
36. Dewan Nurul Anwar Hussain Choudhury: *Jalalabader Katha*, Dacca, 1983, p. 5.
37. Chatterjee, Suniti Kumar: *Origin and Development of Bengali Language,* Calcutta, 1985, Vol. I, p. 202.
38. *Ibid.*, pp. 203-204.
39. Ali, Sayed Murtaza: *Hazrat Shah Jalal O Sylheter Itihas*, Dacca, 1975, p. 203.
40. *Ibid.,* p. 203.
41. *Ibid.*, p. 204.
42. Paul, Bipin Chandra: *Memoirs of My Life and Times,* Calcutta, 1958, Vol. I., p. 27.
43. *Centenary Souvenir*, Govt. H.S. School, Silchar, 1963.
44. Barpujari, H.K.: *Assam in the Days of the Company*, second edition, Gauhati, 1980, p. 190.
45. Hunter,W.W., *op.cit.*, p. 179.
46. *Ibid.*, p. 180.
47. *Ibid.*, pp. 180-81.
48. *Ibid.*, p. 152.
49. *The Englishmen and Military Chronicle*, 22nd Feb. 1858.
50. Chakraborty, Ratan Lal: *Sipahi Juddha O Bangladesh*, Dhaka, 1984, p. 155.
51. *Ibid.*, p. 164. [Letter of Zamindar Bijoy Govinda Choudhury, 19th Dec. 1857. Bangladesh Secretariate Records, Pabna district, Vol. 138, pp. 683-84].
52. Mukharjee, Nilmoni: *A Bengal Zamindar Jay Krishna of Uttarpara and his times, (1808-1838)*, Calcutta, 1975, pp. 190-91.

53. *Ibid.*, p. 191.
45. *Ibid.*, p. 191.
55. *Ibid,* p. 192.
56. *Ibid.*, p. 195.
57. *Ibid.*, p. 195.
58. *Ibid.*, p. 195.
59. *The Hindoo Patriot*, August 20,1857.
60. Gupta, Rajani Kanta: *Sipahi Juddher Itihas*, Calcutta, 1910, Vol. IV, p. 225.
61. Ghosh, Binoy (ed): *Samayik Patre, Bangalar Samaj Chitra*, Calcutta,1982, pp. 389-90.
62. Leonard, A. Gordon, *Bengal: The Nationalist Movement 1876-1940*, London, 1974, p. 2.
63. Chakraborty, Ratan Lal, *op.cit.*, p. 161.
64. Buckland, C.E.: *Bengal Under Lieutenant Governors*, Calcutta, 1901,Vol. II, p. 1029.
65. *Ibid,* Vol. II, p. 1029.
66. Choudhury, Achyut Charan: *Srihatter Itibritta,* Calcutta, 1923, Vol. I, p. 201.
67. Choudhury, Sujit (ed.): *The Mutiny Period in Cachar*, Silchar, 1981, p. 7.
68. Bhattacharjee, Jayanta Bhusan: *The Mutiny in Cachar: A Survey of the Local Sources*, Proceedings of the North East India History Association, Barapani, Shillong, 1983.
69. Guha, Upendra Chandra: *Cacharer Itibritta*, Dacca, 1926, p. 28.
70. Sen, Jyotirmoy: *Untold Story of Mutineers in Cachar*, Raijor Batori, Gauhati, 1975, p. 49.
71. *Bengal Judicial Proceedings*, correspondences of the Magistrate of Sylhet to the Secretary Bengal, 6th Feb., 1858, Calcutta, Vol. I.
72. Chakraborty, Ratan Lal, *op.cit.*, p. 83.
73. Mujmadar, Mujeed Bukht: *The Mujmadar Family of Sylhet*, Sylhet, 1894, p. 9.
74. *Ibid.*, p. 31.
75. *The Dacca News*, 23rd January, 1858, p. 42.
76. Khan, Sarafraj: *The Forgotten Mass Movement of Bengal in the Eighteenth Century*, Dacca, 1970, p. 14.

77. Kar, Subir (ed.): *Mahabidroher Droha Gatha: Jangiyar Geet.*, Calcutta, 2000, p. 59.
78. Joshi Puran Chand.: *1857 in Folk Songs*. [Quoted from Embree, Ainsle T, *1857 in India: Mutiny or War of Independence.*] New Delhi, 1994, p. 12.
79. Joshi, P.C.: *Op.cit.*
80. Mackenzie, Alexander: *The North East Frontier of India*, New Delhi, 1999, p. 369.

Appendices

APPENDIX-A

I. Excerpts of a Few Folk-songs on Maniram Dewan

(a) "*Sonar dhowa khowat khali Ai Maniram*
Rupar dhowa khowat khali,
Kina Ai Raja gharat droha acharili
Dingit Fansi jari lali." ———

— Oh, Maniram happily you were smoking tobacco in the pipes made of gold and silver. What a surprise, you have taken arms in your hands against the British Raj and embraced the glorious death by hanging yourself.

Maniram was hanged in the early part of the morning and his body was kept on the ground uncared for the whole day. The people had witnessed this tragic inhuman act of the British and helplessly lamented and cried:

(b) "*Chalat malangile chaledai kumora*
Tekelit malangile lun
Matit malangile Maniram Dewan ai
Ne kandi thakiba kun".

—Pumpkin has been rotten on the roof, salt has been dissolved into water, like wise Maniram has also been ruined in the hands of the British. Oh! there is none who can check his tears.

(c) *"Firangir bangla sarikoi salia*
Tate bohe firangir mel.
Maniramar khuhanit raj kareng bhangi
Banglat lagale ber."

— Oh, what a strange it is, the encircled Bunglow made of bricks where the Firingis are assembled in the meeting was built by devastating the Raj Kareng (Palace) with the instigation of Maniram.

(d) *"Khiting khiting kora sunilu sabda*
Kinu amongalia katha
Maniram Dewane maidam khandale
Kaknu botora kora."

—The sinister sounds of hammers and crow bars are ringing all around. Oh, whom I will say the unfortunate act of Maniram who demolished the palace into ruins.

(e) *"Bhatiai gale goi kompanir jahajkhan*
Vitare sahor bakas
Deshor dhan sun niye dame dame
Rakhia-paria logat."

—Look, the Ships of the Company are plying on the down stream (on the river Brahmaputra) carrying the golds and jewels of our own country binding in numerous boxes frequently with full arm guards.

(f) *"Atikoi senehar mugare muhura*

Tatokoi senehar maku

Tatokoi sikun Maniram Dewan ai

Nekandi kenekoi thaku?"

— We feel proud of our loveable silk-loom, the spinning shuttle is more loveable, but the loveliest is our Maniram the great. There is none who could refrain himself in lamenting at his tragic end.

(g) *"Jiliye kariba jamur debata*

Kauriye kariba ka

Tinialir murate Maniramak marile

Ubhati boliba ba."

— The chirping of the crickets invite the ominus *Jam,* the God of death; the crow calls the bad omens. Maniram is hanged on the crossing of the three roads, - the wind announces his heroic death.

Quoted from:

1. Goswami, Loke Nath: *'Loka Sangit: Lokayata dhara.'* Loka Charyya, Loka Sanskriti, Guwahati, 1999.
2. Kar, Subir: *Uttar-Purba Bharater Loka Sahitye Bidroha Chetana.' Ibid.,*
3. Gopal Pradhan: *1857 ki anugunj sudur Asom me.*,'Janmat', Patna, Barsha 25, Ank 3,2007, pp. 60-63. (Translated in Hindi from Dutta, Dr. Ajit Kumar: *Maniram Dewan and the Contemporary Assamese Society*.))

II.

Excerpts of a few *BIHU SONGS* on the contents bearing the attitude of the people in the period of Company Rule:

(a) *Companir chakuri na lage kariba*

Nalage golamar dhan

Taro hat dukhani mor o hat dukhani

Duo kari jam ban.

— We do not want to serve in the Company. We do not like to earn money by slavery. Oh my love, we have our own hands to maintain livelihoods.

(b) *Sonarur jalate parai kuruliyai*

Shimulut shen pari raye

Ringi shuni shuni ahiba lahori

Na kariba sipahir bhoye.

— In the golden cage the pegion cries in vain, but the falcon enjoys freedom on the top of the Simul tree. My love, don't afraid of the sipahis, listening the ringing of my bangles come forthwith.

(c) *'Ujaye ahile companir jahaj ai*

prithibi talebalai

Capai de chapai de Ingrejar jahaj ai

Batori achene nai'

—'Up the Brahmmaputra comes the steamer of the English, (it comes) shaking the earth, moor it, moor it, O steamer of the English, is there any news?'

(d) *'Ujai ahile bagichar cahabti*

Cerap khai pelale cica
Atak dhanebastu kehelai lagiche
Chowali nahale micha.,

—'Upstream came the tea-garden Sahib, having drunk he threw away the bottles what's the use of so much wealth all is useless without a woman.'

(e) '*Cahab ahi ahi bagicha khulile*
murat caruhen tupi
kulire chowalik memani karile
mukhate celeudal hupi

— 'The Sahibs come and open up gardens on their heads are pan-shaped topees they make Mems of coolie girls with cigars on their lips.'

[Quoted from, Goswami, Prafulladatta: *Bihu Songs of Assam*, Gauhati, 1957.]

APPENDIX-B

The Treaty between the Raja Gobinda Chandra of Cachar and The East India Company

"Treaty concluded between David Scott, Esquire, agent to the governor general on the part of the honourable East India Company and Rajah Gobind Chunder Narayan, of Cachar or Haramba,- 1825.

Article 1

Rajah Gobind Chunder, for himself and his successors, acknowledges allegiance to the Company, and places his territory of Cachar or Haramba, under their protection.

Article 2

The internal government of the country shall be conducted by the Rajah, and the jurisdiction of the British courts of justice shall not extend there; but the Rajah agrees to attend at all times to the advice offered for the welfare of his subjects by the governor general in council, and agreeably thereto to rectify any abuses that may arise in the administration of affairs.

Article 3

The honourable Company engages to protect the territories of Cachar from external enemies, and arbitrate any differences that may between the Rajah and other states. The Rajah agrees to abide by such arbitration and to hold no correspondence or communication with foreign power except through the channel of the British Government.

Article 4

In consideration of the promised by the above article, and other circumstance, the Rajah agrees to pay to the honourable company, from the beginning of the year 1232

B.S. an annual tribute of ten thousand sicca rupees, and the honourable company engages to provide for the maintenance of the Munnipoorean chiefs lately occupying Cachar.

Article 5

If the Rajah should fail in the performance of the above article, the honourable company will be at liberty, to occupy and attach, in perpetuity, to their other possessions a sufficient tract of the Cachar country to provide for the future realization of the tribute.

Article 6

The Rajah agrees, in concert with British local Authorities, to adopt all measures that may be necessary for the maintenance, in the district of Sylhet, of the arrangements in force in the police, opium, and salt departments. Executed at Budderpore this 6th day of March 1824, corresponding with the 24th of Fagoon 1230 B.S.

Sd/. D. Scott

Agent to the governor general

(-No. XLI Vol II Treaties, Engagements and Sanads.)

Rajah Gobinda Chunder's
Seal.

APPENDIX-C

THE MUJMADAR FAMILY OF SYLHET

A Brief Sketch of Its Members From Surwar Khan to Mujeed Bukht Mujmadar

Printed and Published by K.C. Roy, New Paridarsak Press, Sylhet, 1894

In going back by the traces of recollection and record, to the time when one of our ancestors first made his appearace in this District, I find mention made of him in the person of Surwar Khan. Cabinet Minister to the King Hossain Shah Shurki,whose seat of Government was then at Jaun pore. His visit to this District is associated with a historical event. Gonhur Khan Answari, who in the reign of that King held office with the title of 'Canongo', (Minister), in the place of the Minister Rukan Khan, and held absolute power over Sylhet suddenly died, Bazaad, a Zemindar of Purtabgarh, instigated by his agents Subid Ram and Ram Das who had embezzled certain revenue of the State, atonce declared himself in open rebellion, seized Purtabgarh and Sylhet, and assumed the title of 'Sultan'. Intimation of this having reached the Emperor, Mohammad Khan was sent by him with the title of Minister to assume control of the District in succession to the deceased Gouhar Khan; and Surwar Khan from his knowledge of the District, was deputed not only to quell the rebellion bring the country, people and the property under a proper state of subjection and order, but to regulate and control them to the best of his judgement and discretion on behalf of his royal master.

Surwar Khan arrived in 1464 A.D. and after some fierce engagements the enemy were worsted. Baazeed of Purtabgarh; Sri Shikdar Zemindar of Pergunnah Ita; and Islam Rai, Zemindar of Kanihatti were with difficulty captured. Subid Ram and Ram Das were punished according to their deserts. And, after seeing to order being restored in the District. Surwar Khan returned to the Emperor who rewarded him for his successful zeal and fidelity by appointing his (Surwar Khan's)son. Meer Khan, to the full power of Mohamed Khan over the District of Sylhet. He reigned his lifetime in peace and was succeeded by his son Yusoof Khan to the office of 'Canongoe' He exercised power for many years. When, however, the lineal descendants of Hossain Shah Shurki became extinct, during the revolution following the accession of Sher Shah to the throne of Delhi, Sonaghazi. Kedar Ray and other Zamindars of Bengal, in league with Riasat Aly Khan and Musnad Aly, Zamindars of Jangalbari, Khajah Usman, Khajah Waly and Fata Khan, all acting in consort, by the instigation of Usman and Waly and accompanied by a body of cavalry of certain Afghan rebels against Sher Shah took possession of Pergunnahs Tarfs, Ita and Sylhet where they firmly established themselves and, advised by the nephew (Jadu Ram) of the unprincipled Subid Ram before alluded to, began to practise various sorts of oppression of the lives and property of the people. Certain subadars and soldiers were unsuccessfully despatched by the Emperor to put down the rebellion. Lodi Khan (brother of Yusoof Khan) appeared before the Emperor and acquainted him with the state of affairs in Sylhet. Lodi Khan was then sent in company with Kotboob Uddin, Nazim of Bengal, to Sylhet. The latter was killed in the civil war with Sher Afgan, where upon Lodi Khan returned to the Emperor who conferred on him the title of 'Khan', (Governor), granted him the full power of his father by a Forman of Canongoship and ordered him to proceed with Islam Khan Chisti Nazim of Bengal. Shofat Khan and Mausi Kamal, in war. After several harassing engagements some insurgents, including a body of Afghan cavalry, were captured and order was at length once more restored. Besides certain landed properties such as Nankar and Madadmash lands, etc., granted him rent free. Lodi Khan was allowed by the Emperor Shere Shah to receive tribute at the rate of 5 pies in the rupee, but the Sanads granted him and my other ancestors got burnt. During the time of the East India Company however many Nankar and Madadmash lands &c., were also granted, [Sanad, dated 15th November, 1793] to my grand father Mahmood Bukht.

His presentation to Government in 1857 of 6 pieces of canon with carriage (vide Commissioner of Dacca's letter No. 88 of 12 February 1858, copy of which is here with subjoined:—

From,

The Commissioner of Dacca Division,
To,
The Magistrate of Sylhet,

Sir,

With reference to the accompanying *Urjee* of Haji Sayeed Bukht Mujmadar which was forwarded to me by your predecessor, I have the honour to inform you that His Honour the Lieut. Governor of Bengal considers it desirable to accept the Zamindar's offer of giving up his guns.

You will have the goodness to make arrangement for taking charge from the Sayeed the six small brass guns referred to in the 3rd para of Mr. Heywood's letter to my addres No. 511 of 2nd Nov., 1857. I have, &c,.

The 12th February, 1858.
sd/ W. Allen
Commissioner

These canon originally accompanied his ancestors to quell the rebellion. They had been preserved in the family and were fired on memorable occasions such as the festivals of the Eds, and marriages.

It might not be out of place to mention that we possessed gold and silver maces; 12 mace bearers and a like number of spearmen accompanied us whenever we appeared in public.The maces were disposed of by my father when leaving for Mecca in 1859.

FUTWA

As a special indication of *loyalty* by my father to Her Majesty, I might briefly mention here, that on the eve of his leaving Mecca for India, he caused in 1866 a 'Futwa' (or dispensation of learned Mussulman Doctors and divines) to be drawn up under the Seal and signatures of the muftis of 3 Mussulman sects, Hanafee, Shafe and Malaki (only a limited number of the 4th sect Humbaly being there at the time) to the effect that as here was no interference with Islam under British rule in India, JAHAD (religious war) in opposition to the paramount power in India was not sanctioned by the religion.

On the 23d November 1870, the late Nowab Abdul Latif, Khan Bhadur, C.I.E., convened a public meeting at Calcutta under the patronage of the Hon'ble Sir William Grey, K.C.S.L., Lieutenant Governor of Bengal, with Prince Mohamed Rahim Uddin of the late Mysore dynasty and other personages of note as members. There were present at the meeting amongst others, Kazi Maulavee Abdul Bary, President; Nowab Abdul Latif, Khan Bahadur, Secretary; Moulana Karamat Ali of Jaunpur, Sheik Easa Bina Kirtas, Imteazuddoula, Mirza Ahmed Begg, Khan Bahadur, Samaouddoula, Mohamed

Kasim Ali, Khan Bahadur and others. Several speeches were made and arguments brought forward in support of the above contention, but in as much as the opposers of J A H A D belonged to India, they were apt to be contradicted by persons of the same creed and nationality holding different notions on the subjects. When however, the FUTWAH brought by my father was read by the Secretary, it acted like a charm on the assembly and emanating as it did from Holy Mecca, like oil on the troubled waters soon served to quiet the restless, agitated spirit of the Mussulmans, at a time when learned Moulavees held the opinion that Jahad with the Government was a legitimate object of religion. The FUTWAH's importance was at once admitted and considered the best dispensation that could have been obtained; especially as it was the decision of Muftees an Moulavees of Mecca which could not be questioned or, like that of the laws of the Medes and Persians, was unalterable.

It was clear, and admitted by the Nowab Abdul Latif, that my father's loyalty had served to put down at a stroke a feeling of disloyalty that was beginning to manifest itself at that time.

Appointed Honorary Magistrate, Sylhet, with 3rd class powers,(vide letter No. 410V,S,. dated 21st July 1873) from the Secretary, Government, Bengal, General Department. Received thanks of the Commissioner, Dacca division, (vide Magistrate of Sylhet's No. 863 dated 24th August 1874) for the very creditable and successful arrangements made for reception of the Viceroy on His Excellency's visit to Sylhet.

Appointed Deputy Magistrate and Deputy Collector and posted to the Rajshayee Distrrict (vide No. 1941 C.S. dated 1st. Oct. 1875 from the Secy. Govt. of Bengal).

Served in Bengal for sometime as Deputy Magistrate and Deputy Collector until transferred to Assam as an Extra Assistant Commissioner. Served as such in Sylhet and Silchar. Next posted to the Sub Division of Jorhat in theDistrict of Sibsagar. Served here for 6 or 7 months after which voluntarily resigned the appointment.

Thanks of the Chief Commissioner conveyed in his Secretary's No. 5222 J., dated 31st December, 1889, for assistance rendered in the Lushai Expedition. The letter reads:-

> "I am directed by the Chief Commissioner to tender to you his thanks for the liberal manner in which you supplied fodder for the transport of animals attached to the 43rd Regt. G. L, I., during their march through the Sylhet district and for the supplies of different kinds sent for purchase at the various camps which enable the men of the Regiment to march in greater comfort than would have been the case but for your assistance."

Thanks of the Governor-General of India received through the presidency Magistrate, Calcutta, (vide No. 22 dated 6th February 1890).

Thanks of the Deputy Commissiner, Sylhet for assistance rendered in the Lushai Expedition, (letter No. 7743 dated 22nd February 1890) received through the Sub- divisional Officer, Karimganj.

Thanks of the Chief Commissioner, Assam for assistance rendered in the Lushai Expedition, (vide his Secretary's No. 1829 P, dated 15th May, 1890).

Thanks from the Director of Public Instruction, Assam, (vide hgis No. 1265 dated 20th June 1890) for a gold medal placed at his disposal, to award to the student from Assam standing first in the Entrance Examination that year.

Thanks of the Deputy- Commissioner, Sylhet, (vide No. 4424 dated 11th September 1890), for assistance rendered in treatment of one of the Government elephants.

Thanks of the Brigadier- General (vide his letter dated 27th November 1890) for assistance rendered in the Lushai Expedition.

Acknowledgment dated 6th Jannuary, 1891, from Sir Charles Elliot, Lieutenant-Governor, Bengal of a congratulatory letter on the occasion of his Honor's appointment to the lieutenant Governorship of Bengal.

Allowed to fill up Census Schedules of his family in the same form as Europeans, (vide letter of District Superintendent, Police, dated 28th Jannuary 1891).

Thanks of the chief Commissioner of Assam, conveyed in his Secretary's letter dated 22nd April, 1891, in reply to a letter of condolence with the bereved family of the late Mr. Quinton.

Thanks of the Deputy- Commissioner, Sylhet, (vide No. 2482 dated 3rd July 1891) for assistance rendered in the **Manipur Expedition.**

Acknowledgment in "Assam Gazette" of 22nd August 1891, of Rs 100, subscription to the Quinton Memorial Fund.

Copy of remarks of the Personal Assistance to the Chief Commissioner on the inspection of the Madrassa Syedia dated 32rd December 1819:-

> "Having visited Maulvees Mujeed Bukht Madrassa Sayedia on behalf of the Chief Commissioner, the boys who are all Mohamedaus seem to be well behaved. There are 40 pupils receiving instruction, Arabic and Persian"

Invitation to a Ball given by Sir Cecil and Lady Beudon on 16th February 1867.

Invitation to a Ball given by the Lieutenant Governor on 30th December 1868.

An invitation by the Countess of Mayo request the pleasure of Hajee Mujeed Bukht's company on Monday afternoon the 3rd Jannuary from 4 o' clock. Garden party.

Invitation by the Lieutenanat- Governor of Bengal, to meet H.E.the Viceroy and H.R.H. the Duke of Edinburgh, at an Evening party, on 1st Jannuary 1870.

Invitation from H.R.H. to meet the viceroy at a Ball on H. M's *Man-Of-War Galatea*, on 4th Jannuary. A copy of the letter is subjoined:-

> To have the honor of meeting His Excellency the Viceroy. The Equerry in waiting is commanded by His Roal Highness the Duke of Edinburgh to request the company of Hajee Mujeed Bukht to a Ball on board H.M.S. Galatea on Tuesday evening 4th Jannuary at half past nine O' clock. *Full dress.*

Thanks of Her Imperial Majesty and H.R.H. Prince and princess of Wales and Royal Family (conveyed in Secretary to Chief Commissioner's No. 573 dated 17th February 1892) for the kind sympathy express on the death of H.R.H.Prince Albert Victor of Wales, Duke of Clarence and Avondale.

Thanks of Sir Dennis Fitzpatrick, lieutenant Governor of the Punjub, conveyed in the Private Secretary's letter dated 7th March 1892.

I might be permitted to add that owing to our sincere loyalty our kind Government still favors us as hithertofore by accepting our humble invitation. The last invitation the chief Commissioner was pleased to accept was on 3rd Jannuary 1894 when he, with the local European ladies and gentlemen, official and non-official, was pleased to grace my humble abode with his presence at a Tea Party.

APPENDIX-D

The Diary of Mr. Brenand, the Principal of Dacca College and an Eye Witness of the Incidents in the Mutiny Period

"The mutinies began at Barrackpore in March, 1857, by the 34th N.I. (Native Infanty). Three officers were wounded. The 19th at Berhampore then showed signs of disaffection: they were ordered to Barrackpore, and both regiments were disbanded.

"In May news arrived of the outbreak at Meerut. At this time the sepoys stationed at Dacca consisted of two companies of the 73rd N.I. In this month the Missionaries met with some opposition from the sepoys, whilst preaching in the Bazaar.

At the end of May, or beginning of June, two other companies of the 73rd arrived from Julpigoree as a relief for those that had been in Dacca for some time.

"10th June- the troops appear excited on account of the rumour that European troops are to be sent to Dacca.

"June 12th – a panic spread among the Europeans, in consequence of a report, to the effect that the two companies of the 73rd, which had left the station about the beginning of the month, had met with some disbanded men from Barrackpore, and had mutinied: that they had returned to Dacca, and had been joined by the men at the Lal Bagh: that they were looting the Bazaar, and setting free the prisoners at the Jail.

A number of Europeans assembled at the house of Mr. Jenkins the Magistrate; others resolved to defend themselves at the bank. Some of the ladies went on board boats on the river: arms were collected: the whole town was in a state of excitement: the bund was crowded with Natives in a state of wonder and curiosity.

Lieutenant Mc Mohan and Ryn, the officers in command of the troops, started for the Lal Bagh, where the sepoys wre located. On their return they reported that their men were all quiet and in their quarters: that the alarm was groundless.

On the evening drive, the Natives who were collected in knots along the road seemed surprised to see us, after the report that we had all fled, and left them to their fate.

13TH – Everything quiet again, and we are going on with our work as usual.

Between the 19th and, 23rd June, the government sent up a hundred men of the Indian Navvy, under Lieutenant Lewis, for the protection of the town. They were located in the house on the opposite side of the road to the Baptist Chapel.

28th- two deserters were caught in the neighbourhood by the police, but were rescued by some of the sepoys. The two companies were paraded, but the burkundazes either could not point out the men who had assisted in the rescue, or they were afraid to do so. The sepoys complained that they could not go about the town without being interfered with by the police.

5th July- the Metcalfes came in from Comillah in a fright: they had heard that the sepoys at Chittagong had mutinied, and that they were on their way to Dacca. The report was, however, without foundation.

Dacca has been comparatively quiet since the arrival of the sailors. Lieutenant Lewis has his tars out frequently in the morning to practise with the guns in the space near the Racquet Court, and infront of the college. He wheels his men about in all directions: sometimes he storms the collectorate, first at one gate, then at the other, going through all the manoeuvers for loading and firing. The sepoys on guard are very angry: they say yih kia dar dekhlate? They do not seem to have much affection for the sailors.

Today there was something of a panic among the sepoys. Dowell who is in command of the station, sent upto the Lal Bagh for the screws used in elevating the guns, and the men there supposed that there was some intention of disarming them.

30th July-a meeting of European and East Indian inhabitants capable of bearing arms was held at the college: nearly 60 peop'e present. It was resolved to form two corps of volunteers, one of Infantry and the other of Cavalry. Major Smith to command the Infantry, and Lieutenant Hitchins the Cavalry.

1st, 2nd, and 3rd August–the three days of Buckree Eed. The volunteers all on the alert: patrols out all night on each of three days. Apprehension that the Mahomedans may cause some disturbance. The 2nd being Sunday, a party of the volunteer stationed at the college to protect the people who were at Church. Great alarm amongst the European and Armenian residents, especially among with families. The terrible news from the North- West proves the necessity of being prepared for any sudden outbreak.

11th August- many of the Armenians are leaving for Calcutta. The Europeans are thinking of fortifying the mills. The volunteers are on parade for several hours daily and are making good progress in drill. File firing tomorrow and target practice shortly. The natives scarcely understand the commotion among the Sahib, or the object of the 'Volunteer ka pultan', who have been keeping up nightly patrols.

14th and 15th August- the festival of the Junme Ostemee. There was as usual a large crowd of people. The Cavalry volunteers weer mounted on elephans and well armed and ready for anything that might occur.

The Infantry were also armed, and at the college, but all passed off quietly. Letters from Julpigoree, the Head Quarters of the 73rd. The officers say they have no hope of being able to keep their men from following the example of the rest of the Bengal Army. They have sent away two of the Ensigns to Darjeeling: but that if their men should rise, they have no expectation of being able to escape as the country is completely inundated; and they have no pucka house in which they could take refuge to defend themselves.

It has been decided that if the men at Julpigoree do mutiny, the sepoys here shall be at once disarmed.

There are about 50 men at the collectorate: and the plan will be to disarm these in the first instance, and afterwards to proceed to the Lal Bagh to disarm the men there, and to bring away the guns now in their charge.

22nd August- the fortification of the mills is going on: and it will not be long before the place will be ready. There are 200 men at work, digging a ditch from the nullah round the house to the river.

27th August- the fortifications are progressing; and it is supposed that should there be occasion for it, we should be able to make a stand against firve or six thousand men. The country around is, however, quiet, but there are many rumours of armed men having been seen at different places coming down the river in boats.

We are informed by the Magistrate that we are to have two companies of Europeans at Dacca, and one troop of house Artillery, within a month.

30th August- Yeesterday, Sunday, was the great day of the **Mohurrum.** The cavalry volunteers weer out all night patrolling; they describe the town as unusually quiet. The people did not assemble in the same numbers as in former years. Only about 50 were present at the **Hosseinee Dalan**. It is believed that the Musalmans are completely cowed.

14th September- some alarm here in consequence of a report that the sepoys in Assam are in a state of great excitement, and that they had become very insolent. The government has sent off a number of sailors in the Horungatta by way of the Sunderbuns; they are expected to arrive here tomorrow, and are intended for Assam.

The 73rd at Julpigoree still quiet. We have hoped that it will prove staunch. Should it not, we shall be involved here; but we shall be quiet a mutch for more respectful towards us of late.

27th September- everything quiet. The apprehensions regarding the spread of the insurrection to Bengal are in measure allayed.

4th October- to day has been fixed upon by the Bishop as a day of humiliation. Winchester away at Sylhet. The service was read by Abercromje, and the sermon by Pearson. In Dacca we are all quiet. The Rajah* of Assam was the brought in a prisoner in the day before yesterday.

12th October- the cavalry volunteers gave a ball to the Infantry. The gathering not so great as was expected; about 10 ladies present. Of the Infantry volunteers only 20 attended in uniform. The party was, on the whole, a very pleasant one.

19th October- some of the sepoys here have been recently punished, but the matter has been kept quiet.

November 1st - something like a panic occurred on Sunday last, caused by the removal of the sailors to the house near the Church recently occupied by the Nuns. The sepoys got ammunition out of the magazine; and it was thought that an outbreak was imminent. It is reported that they have written to their brethren at Julpigoree, asking whether they should resist if an attempt were made to disarm them. We believe that the disarming could be effected with little danger to ourselves; but it is feared that the effect on the troops at Chittagomg. Sylhet, and Julpigoree might be disastrous. It is supposed that if we can preserve order in Dacca, the other plces will remain quiet. The men are very civil, but with the example of their 'bhai buns' before us, we cannot put much trust in them.

9th November- the Infantry volunteers gave a dinner to the station. It came off in the large hall of my house. It was one of the largest parties of gentlmen that has ever been in Dacca. About seventy were invited, and upwards of fifty sat down to dinner. People thought that my house would not be large enough for the occasion, but everything was very convenienty arranged.

17th November- everything continues quiet around us, and the news from the North-West is more cheering.

26th – the storm that has been passing over India has just passed Dacca, happily, without any of the disastrous effects that have attended it in its course elsewhere. We are now rid of our 'Staunch' and 'Loyal' friends–the sepoys. Up to Saturday last we are going on just as usual. There was party out at cricket in the afternoon, and the volunteers' were at their usual exercise with ball cartridge. In the evening we had our usual drive on the course. The dwak, however, brought bad news from Chittagong; and an express was received with intelligence that the remnant of the 34th, the regiment disbanded at Barrackpore at the beginning of the mutiny had broken out; that they had looted the Treasury, taking with them about three lakhs of rupees; and that they had also killed several Europeans. It is now believed that the Europeans escaped. At about 6 O'clock in the evening, it was determined that the sepoys here the Artilery men under the command of Dowell, was 260. They had possession of two field pices; and in their blines they held remarkably strong position. It is reported that they threatened to resist any attempt at disarming them, and they affected to despise our sailor who are generally of small stature. The sailors were about 90 in number, fit for duty. It was therefore necessary that they should use great precautions in dealing with a body of armed men, nearly three times their number.

The volunteers were warned to be ready at 5 o'clock the following morning, Sunday, the 22nd and they were enjoined to assemble quietly, so as to excite no suspicion.

At the time appointed, there were assembled the commissioner, the Judge, and some other civilians, and from twenty to thirty volunteers. It was still dark, and we waited a short time for the signal. The plan was, to being by disarming the Treasury guard, to place the disarmed men in charge of the volunteers; sailors would then proceed with their whole force to the Lal Bagh; and it was hoped that the men there would have given up their arms without opposition. Everything appeared to go on well; the guards at the Treasurey were disarmed before the signal was given for the volunteers to advance. There were about fifteen of them making altogather about 36, were supposed to be inside the building. They appeared to be very much dejected, and they reproached their officers for subjecting them to such disgrace, protesting that they would have given up their arms at once to their own officers had they only been asked to do so.

'In the meantime, the sailors. On reaching the Lal Bagh, found the sepoys drawn out, prepared to make a resistance; they had evidently been apprised of our intention to disarm them. The sentry fired his musket and killed one of our men; his example was followed by the others, and a volley was fired on the sailors as they advanced through the broken wall near the Southern gateway. The guns had been placed in position in front of Beebee Peri's tomb, so as to command the entrance, and they opened fire upon our men with grape. As soon as the sailors had go well into the place, they fired a volley. Lieutenant Lewis then led them up the ramparts to the left, charging the sepoys, and drivin them before at the point of the bayonet. The sepoys took shelter in their quarters, but they were driven on from building to building by the sailors. At this time Mr. Mays, a midshipman, at the head of eight men who were under his command, made a gallant charge from the ramparts down upon the sepoy guns; they were soon taken and spiked, and the sepoys began flying in every direction. There was a severe struggle at the end of the rampart; many of the sepoys were driven over the parapet. Mr. Bainbridge had also a fall over the parapet as he stepped back to avoid the thrust of one of the sepoys. The sailors obtained a complete victory; the sepoys field and concealed themselves in the jungle, leaving about forty of their number killed. Many of those who escaped were severely wounded. Our loss was one killed on the field, four severely wounded, since dead and nine more or less severely wounded. Dr. Green, who accompanied the sailors, was wounded in thigh. He was kneeling down at the time attending to one of the sailors, who had also been wounded. He is gegetting on well, but complains of numbnees in the lower parts of leg.

A number of the fugitive sepoys have been brought in. Four of them have been already hung, and several others are to undergo the same punishment.

On Monday everything was quiet again, and we were going on with our work as if nothing had happened. But many of the natives left the city through fear.

29th November- we have had great apprehensions during the week regarding the residents at Mymensing and Sylhet. It has been ascertained that our fugitive sepoys were on their way towards those places.

It is fortunate, however, that they are not all proceeding together. The largest party only took the Toke road towards Mymensing, about twenty of their armed men were in front, then followed some of the disarmed men and only one woman with her children; then the wounded, who appear to have been numerous, and lastly, another body of about thirty armed men.

As they approached Mymensingh, the Magistrate, with a number of burkundazes, took the field to oppose their passing through the station. They declined the fight and took the direction to Jamalpore.

The Chittagong mutineers were on their way to Dacca, and it was supposed that their object was to join the men of the Seventy-third. It was then reported that they were about to cross the Tipperah hills to join the men stationed at Sylhet. It is now currently reported that they are at a place on the other side of Comillah; that they have sent a massage to the Rajah of Tipperah, that if he dose not join them they will dethrone him. The European inhabitants of Comillah, and the respectable native inhabitants, have all got away.

30th November,- three of the Lal Bagh mutineers were hung this morning; these, with eight others that have already undergone the same punishment, make eleven in all. We consider that such examples are absolutely necessary in these times. They have produced an excellent effect upon the people, and the bad characters of the town thoroughly understand the lesson that has been read to them. I do not remember the time when the natives were so civil in their behaviour as they are now.

3rd December, - two steamers and a flate arrived this morning with 300 of the 54th Queen's Regiment and 100 sailors on board. The soldiers start for the Tipperah district as soon as sufficient stock of provisions can be collected. It is supposed that they will be in time to intercept the men from Chittagong before they can reach Sylhet. The sailors will proceed to Bulwah on their way to Rungpore. It is to be hoped they are not too late.

The Sylhet **dawk** is stopped. It is supposed that the Chittagong mutineers are somewhere on the Sylhet road.

9th December- the latest reports from Sylhet state that the Chittagong mutineer had not reached that station; that they were somewhere in the territories of the Rajah of Tipperah;

and that they were afraid to venture upon the plains for fear of the **gora log**. Their party in all consisted of about 500, including their women and children, and the prisoners they had set free the gaol at Chittagong. They were in great want of provisions, and were stockading themselves, expecting an attack to be made upon them.

18th December- No tidings for the last few days from Sylhet. The last news received was to the effect that the people there were prepared to give the mutineers a warm reception if they should venture upon attacking them. We hope to hear shortly from the troops, which left us so lately.

The Dacca mutineers are supposed to be somewhere in Bhootan.

14th January, 1858- The station is now somewhat gay. The steamers with the European troops have returned. The Chittagong mutineers had kept too close to the jungle on their way to Sylhet. The Sylhet Light Infantry came up with them on two occasions, and each time they have beaten them.

The soldiers and sailors are strolling about the streets in great numbers. There is some uncertainty if they are to remain at Dacca. The general impression is that they are not required here, and that they might be usefully employed elsewhere.

24th January- the European troops have left for Calcutta. Although everything is quiet on this side of the country, the sailors will probably remain for several months longer.

The principle topic now in India is the transfer of the Gocverment to the Crown, and the probable changes that may take place in the different services, and in the general interests of the country.

17th March- every thing has settled down to the usual quite which prevailed before the mutinies. The government has been contemplating the laying down a telegraphic line between Calcutta and Chittagong via Dacca. A number of people have arrived in connection with the Telegraph Department; they have pitched their tents on the triangular space of ground before the church.

3rd April- the scheme of a Railway to Dacca, which was before the public in 1856, is again attracting much attention and may not be long before the line is commenced.

30th May- there is a rumour that 500 European troops are to be located at Dacca.

9th June- on Saturday last, Davidson, the Commissioner, sent me a copy of an extract from the proceedings of the president in council, ordering that the college building should be prepared immediately for the accommodation of a wing of the 19th Regiment, consisting of four hundred and fifty men. Those that cannot be accommodated in the students leave for ten days, or a fortnight, till another building can be procured for their use.

27th June- I have received the sanction of Government to take two houses for the use of the college during the time that the college building may be occupied by the Military.

12th July- three companies of the 19th Europeans have arrived; the greater number will be located in the college, the others will occupy the **Foujadaree** court.

The station is very gay. A ball at **Gunny Meeah's**, a station ball at Carnegie and bachelor's ball after that.

The public garden South of the college has been made

over to a joint stock company, for the purpose of building assembly rooms library theatre, billiard room etc,. etc.

1ST August- the sailors started for Sylhet yesterday.

15th August- the station is very gay. Three balls in succession.

18th October- Telegraphic line completed between Calcutta and Dacca. The question of a railway still under consideration.

5th November- the proclamation of the transfer of the government of India to the Queen was read in English and Bengali on Monday last, in the space in front of the college. The Military were drawn up in line and the European residents were upon a platform erected for the purpose. Between two or three thousand people present. Some of the houses were lighted up in the evening in honor of the occasion, and there was a dinner given by the Civilians and Military to the station.

"The students had an illumination at the college with fireworks the following evening; they seemed quite enthusiastic in the display of their loyality".

[Clay , A.L., *Principal Heads of the History and Statistics of Dacca Division* (London, 1868), pp. 40-47.]

APPENDIX-E

1. The name of the *Aulias*, the followers of Hazrat Shah Jalal:

[Quoted from, Choudhury, Achyut Charan: *Srihatter Itibritta*, Vol. II, pp. 38-44]

1. Abdul Aziz
2. Abdul Ali (Shekh)
3. Abdullah (Shekh)
4. Abdul Karim (Shekh)
5. Abdul Jalil
6. Abdul Malique
7. Abdul Sukkur
8. Abdulla Saheb
9. Abdul Hakim
10. Abdus Sakar
11. Abdus Rahim
12. Abbas (Sayed)
13. Abu Bakkar Sani (Sayed)
14. Abul Khayer
15. Abul Aziz
16. Abu Bakkar (Sayed) / Pargana Chhotlekha, Karimganj
17. Abul Fazal (Shekh)
18. Abul Hassan
19. Abu Torab / Bandar bazaar, Sylhet
20. Abu Saheed
21. Adam Khakhi
22. Ahmed Abbasi

23. Ahmed Nessar Bardaar
24. Ahmed Saheb (Shekh)
25. Ahmed Kabir (Sayed)
26. Ahmed (Sayed)
27. Ahmed (Sayed)
28. Ajiuddin Khaza Saheb
29. Aziz (Sahid)
30. Azimuddin Kazi
31. Aziwan (Sayed)
32. Ali Emoni
33. Ali Emoni Shahjada (Shekh) / Dargah of Shah Jalal, Sylhet
34. Alim (Sayed)
35. Ameer (Sayed)
36. Amanullah (Shekh)
37. Arif Multani
38. Arez Ashkari
39. Ataullah Hafiz
40. Badaruddin (Sayed)
41. Badar (Shahid)
42. Badar Maleque
43. Ba- Abu Daulat / Pargana Chhankhair, Sylhet.
44. Bagdar Ali Shah / Barudkhana, Sylhet.
45. Baaz (Shekh)
46. Baazid (Sayed)
47. Bahauddin (Shekh)
48. Bahar Ashkari

49. Boz Burg (Sayed)
50. Burhan Uddin Burhana
51. Burhan Uddin Ketan (Khaza)
52. Chand Shah /Chand bharang, Sylhet
53. Chasni Pir /Gowairpara, Sylhet town.
54. Chat or Chet Shah / Near Govt. School, Sylhet.
55. Daud Bakhs Khatib
56. Daud Qureshi /Pargana Renga, Sylhet.
57. Dada Pir/Sylhet
58. Daur Bax Khateeb
59. Delaor Khateeb
60. Daulat Gani
61. Daulat Gazi
62. Daulat Neeri
63. Daulat (Sayed)
64. Daulat (Shahid0
65. Dud Maleque
66. Etim Shah / Badur latka, Sylhet town.
67. Emam Uddin
68. Emam Sukurullah
69. Ehiya Kkari
70. Fakruddin (Sayed)
71. Fakkaruddin (Kazi)
72. Fazula (Kazi)
73. Farid Saheb (Sayed)
74. Farid Ansari (Shekh)
75. Farid Rousan Berag

76. Firoz Atayi
77. Firoz (Kazi)
78. Fayazuddin (Shekh)
79. Fateh Gazi Saheb / Pargana Taraf, Sylhet.
80. Gani Pir
81. Garib Khaki
82. Garib (Shekh)
83. Gazi Manek
84. Habib Gazi
85. Hafez Fasi
86. Hafez Mohammad
87. Haji Ahammad
88. Haji Ahammad
89. Haji Gazi / Edgah Maidan, Sylhet town.
90. Haji Kasem
91. Haji Khalil/ Sylhet town.
92. Haji Khizir
93. Haji Latif
94. Haji Mohammad
95. Haji Mohammad Omsed
96. Haji Mohammad Zakaria
97. Haji Mohammad Daraiah
98. Haji Mohammad Sarif
99. Haji Omar Chisti
100. Haji Osman Dauri
101. Haji Yusuf /Sylhet town.
102. Hazarat Golam /Jallar par, Sylhet town.

103. Hazarat Jalaluddin (Saheed)
104. Hazarat Jahan / Jallar par, Sylhet town.
105. Hazarat Jahan (Sayed)
106. Hazarat Jehan (Kazi)
107. Hazarat Dewan Fateh Mahmud
108. Hazarat Lal
109. Hazarat Lal (Sayed)
110. Hazarat Mohammad Shahial
111. Hazarat Abu Fazal
112. Hazarat Karam Mohammad (Shekh)
113. Hazarat Kalu Shah
114. Hamid Farooki / Kanihati, Sylhet.
115. Hamiduddin Nurnari
116. Hamzah (Shaheed)/ Sylhet.
117. Hasem Chisti
118. Helim uddin Behari
119. Helim uddin (Shekh) / Pargana Kanihati, Sylhet.
120. Hesam uddin Behari
121. Humanuddin
122. Hussain (Shekh)
123. Hussain (Shaheed) / Sylhet town.
124. Hussain (Shaheed)
125. Hussain (Suffi)
126. Huzzat uddin Behari
127. Huzzat Maleque
128. Hybatullah Khateeb
129. Hayder Gazi / Sylhet

130. Ilrash (Sheikh)
131. Isha (Sheikh)
132. Isha (Sayed)
133. Ismail Omari
134. Jakaria Arbi
135. Jakaria Hafez
136. Jakai (Shekh) / Kazi tola, Sylhet town.
137. Jayanuddin
138. Jayanuddin Abbasi
139. Jalaludin (Kaji) / Kazi tola, Sylhet town.
140. Jalil (Sayed)
141. Jamaluddin
142. Jamal (Shekh)
143. Jahangir (Shahid)
144. Jawhar (Shahid)
145. Jhakmak (Khanda)
146. Jinda Pir / Jinda bazar, Sylhet.
147. JiyauddinMohammad(Shekh)/ Deorail Pargana, Krimganj.
148. Jiyauddin (Shekh) / Pnch Pirer Mokam,Sylhet town.
149. Jiyaullah
150. Joned Gujrati
151. Kabir (Sayed)
152. Karimdad rumi
153. Kamaludin / Pargana Chuallish, Sylhet.
154. Kamal Emoni
155. Kalamiya

156. Kalu Shah Pir/ Pirer gram, Sylhet
157. Kasem (Sayed)
158. Kasem dakshini (Sayed)
159. Kutubuddin (Sheikh)
160. Kutub Alam
161. Kutubuddin (Sayed)
162. Khalilullah (Shahid)
163. Khalil Dewana
164. Khaza Aiz Chisti
165. Khaza Aziuddin
166. Khaza Aad
167. Khaza Aadena
168. Khaza Amiruddin
169. Khaza Ali
170. Khaza Essa
171. Khaza Essa Chisti
172. Khaza Ekbal
173. Khaza Ekhtiar
174. Khaza Omar Jahan
175. Khaza Omar Chisti
176. Khaza Taiyar
177. Khaza Daud
178. Khaza Nasirudin
179. Khaza Piyeer
180. Khaza Bahaudin
181. Khaza Maleque
182. Khaza Shiraz

183. Khaza Saalim
184. Khaza Sufiana
185. Khizir Khastdabir (Sheikh) / Sylhet town.
186. Khizir Suffi /Barud khana, Sylhet town.
187. Lal Saheb /Sadagar tolah, Sylhet town.
188. Madsuddin [Madu Sudan] / Rekabi bazaar, Sylhet town.
189. Maghud Maleque
190. Mahabat (Sayed) / Pargana Mahurapur, Sylhet
191. Maheb Ali
192. Mahiuddin
193. Makaddum Saheb
194. Makaddum Saheb
195. Makaddum Saheb
196. Makaddum Saheb/ Prgana Kanihati, Sylhet
197. Makaddum Habib / Pargana Kanihati, Sylhet
198. Makaddum Jafar Gaznavi / Pargana Kanihati, Sylhet
199. Makaddum Nezamuddin Osmani
200. Makaddum Rahimuddin / Pargana Jalalpur, Sylhet
201. Malek Mohammad
202. Maruf Heladar
203. Manayim (Sayed)
204. Maouddur
205. Mokhtar (Sayed)/ Sylhet town.
206. Mohammad Amin
207. Mohammad Ansari (Sheikh)

208. Mohammad Asheikh
209. Mohammad Ayub Emam
210. Mohammad Gaznavi (Sayed)
211. Mohammad Iasin
212. Mohammad Janedi
213. Mohammad Jahan
214. Mohammad Kerabi(Sheikh)
215. Mohammad Saleh
216. Mohammad Selahdar
217. Mohammad Selahudar
218. Mohammad Taqui
219. Mohammad Dana (Sheikh)
220. Mohammad Noor
221. Mohammad Rousan (Sayed)
222. Mohammad Latif
223. Mohammad Behari
224. Mohammad Sahabani
225. MojaffarBehari
226. Moqtar (Shahid)
227. Moulana Quamuddin
228. Musa (Sheikh)
229. Musa Abdul Ali (Shahid)
230. Mustafa (Shahid)
231. Nar Naoli
232. Nasarullah
233. Nasiruddin Sipah-I-Salar (Sayed)
234. Nezamuddin Boddadi

235. Nezamuddin Kromani
236. Neamatullah (Sheikh)
237. Nur Ali
238. Nurul Huda
239. Nurul Huda
240. Nur Maleque
241. Nurullah
242. Nusrat (Sheikh)
243. Omar (Sheikh)
244. Omar (Sheikh)
245. Omar Chisti
246. Omar Darwari
247. Omar (Kaji)
248. Omar Samarkhandi (Shahid)/Dhopa dighir par, Sylhet.
249. Osman Sahib
250. Osmanuddin
251. Osman (Sheikh)
252. Osman (Sayed)
253. Osmanuddin
254. Parbat Jahan Saheb
255. Pir Amin Saheb
256. Pir Amin Saheb(follower)
257. Pir Dariya /Sylhet town.
258. Pir Jahan Saheb
259. Pir Malek / Graveyard, Sylhet town.
260. Pir Manek (follower) /Graveyard, Sylhet town.

261. Pir Panchatan/ the grave of Pauch Pir, Sylhet town.
262. Ruknuddin Ansari / Pargana Sarail, Sylhet.
263. Ruknuddin (Sayed)
264. Saams (Sheikh)
265. Saabu (Sheikh)
266. Sadar Sheikh
267. Sad-Ha (Sheikh)
268. Sahabaz Ansari
269. Saleh Maleque
270. Salim (Sheikh)
271. Sarafuddin (Sheikh)
272. Sarif Azmiri
273. Sayefuddin (Sayed)
274. Sayed Lal / Kuarpar, Sylhet town.
275. Shah Dewan (Kaji)
276. Shah Farang or Shah Darrang /Manumukh, Maulavibajar.
277. Shah Kamal / Shar para, Sylhet town.
278. Shah Madan / Tilagarh, Sylhet.
279. Shah Malum / Pargana Mahurapur, Sylhet.
280. Shah Noor / Bandar bazaar, Sylhet town.
281. Shah Paran / Pargana Dakshin Kachh, Sylhet.
282. Shah Rafiuddin/Shah Rafing, Sylhet.
283. Shah Sadaruddin / Pargana Bade Satarasati, Sylhet.
284. Shah Sajjar/ Barud khana, Sylhet.
285. Shah Samsuddin / Mouza Sayed pur, Sylhet.

286. Shah Sikandar Gazi Sultan./ Sylhet.
287. Shah Sikandar mohammad / Pargana Chhan Khair, Sylhet.
288. Shah Sundaar / Prgana Dakshin Kachh, Sylhet.
289. Sheikh Kalu
290. Sikandar Mohammad
291. Sikandar (Sheikh)
292. Sikandar Tablabaz
293. Sirajuddin (Sheikh)
294. Sohabuddin
295. Sona Gazi (Sheikh)
296. Sultan Shah(Sayed)
297. Taher(Sheikh)
298. Taiyaf Salami / Pargana Godhrali. Sylhet.
299. Tajuddin /
300. Tajuddin Shah (Sahid)/ Aorangpur
301. Taj Maleque
302. Yeakub (Sayed)
303. Yusuf (Sayed)

The name of the other 57 Nos. Followers of Hazarat Shahjalal are presently not available. Historians are of the opinion that, "After the death of Shah Jalal, the district (Sylhet) was included in the kingdom of Bengal and put in charge of a Nabab."

[Principal Heads of the History and Statistics of the Dacca Division p. 291. Quoted in, *Srihatter Itibritta*,Choudhury Achyut Charan.]

THE HEROIC BALLAD OF THE MUTINY

JANGIYAR GEET

Hymn:

The Rising sun in the East
I venerate,
Whose appearance illumes the Earth.

[Oh, the ordeal of Allah is befalling us.]

The Northern shrine, and the deities in
the pantheon, I venerate.
The Holy shrine of Mecca-Hindustan
In the West, I venerate,
My greetings to all the non-Hindus.

Oh, great Kalidaha, a lump of iron
reaches your bottom in six months,
I venerate you, you occupy the earth in North.

All the Messengers of Holy Allah,
I venerate.
My mother, I venerate your feet,
All the mendicants I venerate
And send my humble salutation to all.
I offer greetings to my mother
And I worship you Goddess Saraswati,
Lord Ganapati, I invoke you
In this platform [to bless me.]

[Oh, the ordeal of Allah is befalling us.]

Mother Saraswati, the goddess of learning

Who offered me her lap
In my childhood,
I seek your blessings.
Do not forsake me in my old age.
I call upon you, mother Saraswati,
To bless me in my voice,
To tune me for rendering
The grand verse [of the Holy warriors.]
My mother, why should you forsake me
And bestow all your favours to Kartika and Ganesha.

[Oh, the ordeal of Allah is befalling us.)

With all my heart and soul
I invoke Holy Allah,
I worship the Four directions
The North South and East and West.

I touch your feet with gratitude,
By your grace,
I am now here to render my song.
I greet Allah, the Almighty,
Mother Fatema,
Hassan and Hussain also I greet.
The messengers of Lord,
All the ambias, the mendicants all
And my parents I greet with
All solemnity.
Everybody present here,
All my co religious brethren too I greet.

Mother, [the goddess of learning]

Be in my voice, and grace me in my venture.
I will render the verse in my humble voice
And try to render as much as I am capable of.

[Oh, the ordeal of Allah is befalling us.]

The Story:
A man there was in Chittagong,
He was called Mugal,
Allah blessed him with five offsprings.
To Madrasa he sent them all
But the four came back home
Leaving only one to study the scripture
and to become a Hafiz.
He studied eight years
and on completion
he dreamt his mother's crying in one night.
Waking up, he prayed to God
and recited Koran in great fear.

[Oh, the ordeal of Allah is befalling us.]

He then went to his master
the master, on completion of
prayer and recitation, desired to know
Why the visit.
The Hafiz touched his master's feet and
began to shed tears.
Consoling the boy the master
Wished to hear everything in details.

'Here my master, I submit before you

as I am yours since I am eight
last night I had a dream,
my mother is in tears.
Allow me, my master, to
go home and see my mother for once'.
—'Go my son, I bid you 'bye
go home, stay for three or four days
and then come back.'

Saluting the master's feet
the Hafiz made for his home.
The four brothers received him in the house
And the message was sent to the mother.

[Oh, the ordeal of Allah is befalling us.]

The ordeal of Allah is befalling us
The calamity is impending on the warriors.
Recite ye all, the verses of Koran
With all your heart and soul.

The mother then rushed forward
the son touched the feet with
tears in his eyes.
—'My son, how could you bear
the pang of separation
you never had time to
return for eight long years.'

—'My mother, forgive me.
But you have four sons left by the grace of Allah.
Leave me to the madrasa
to serve Allah

and to seek His blessings
for the day of the final judgement.

—My mother, tell me
where has gone my father?
—he's in the town of Nagarpur
and in the service of the government.

—Mother, my dear mother,
For Allah's sake, tell me, what is he?

—Listen, my son,
Yours father 's a police man.

—Oh mother! Hafiz began to cry,
the earning livelihood from this service
is a sinful act
The Holy Koran forbids it.
Please mother, let my father be
called back home.
Write a letter to him now
And I will hand it over to the postman.'

The letter was written -
Hafiz too added and wrote a few words
desiring to see the father,

—'when you will receive this
think my father, the food and
water of your place shall become unholy.

Mugal woke up
And made the prayer as usual
The Postman came

and delivered the letter to him
Mugal read and realized with a heavy heart –
The food and the water of the city unholy to him.
He took the letter to his master
The sahib granted leave
—'Your son is back
after eight years,
—go home and stay for
a couple of days'.

In the name of Allah
Mugal made for home.
The five sons greeted him
with reverence.
He entered house happily then
with five sons Mugal sat to dine.
As they just finished the half of the meal
Hafiz spoke to his father:

'I wished to remind you, father,
Koran forbids the service in police,
You have five offspring by the grace of Allah
Why not stay home and
work together to earn.

—If that's not enough, my father
I'll maintain by begging even,
For Allah's sake, resign the job now.'
Listening to the son Mugal
stopped eating and spoke thus
to son:

—'Oh, you have had a little learning
and you've out moralizing your father
I won't have you return to
Madrasa any more.'

Getting up with anger, Mugal
straightway rushed for Nagarpur
putting on the police attire
appeared before the officer
and salute.

Asked the officer,
- you sought leave for eight days
what caused you to return so soon?

Mugal narrated in details and requested,
—Sir, please send some sepoys
to fetch my insolent boy.

The Sahib then convinced
and sent sepoys for the arrest of Hafiz.

Meanwhile the son appeared at Nagarpur
on his own.
To Omar Khalifa Hafiz placed a
demand for police uniform.

Omar the tailor, got surprised and
requested him,
—you should go back to
study the Holy scripture instead.

—Hey, cloth – maker,
my father is in a row with me

and must have sent the force
to put me to the jail.

The Khalifa then stitched
the police- attire,
and supplied a gun
chanting the Holy verses
Hafiz hurriedly returned.

On the way Mugal
and the English sepoys
fell upon Hafiz.
The son lost the battle
jumped into the sea
and boarded a ship secretly
bound for Chittagong.

Oh, the Ordeal of Allah is befalling us.
The ship's landed on Chittagong
listened to the morning prayer
Hafiz entered the mosque near by
met one Subedar there, who asked
him where from he had come.
Hafiz related his sad tale and begged shelter
Subedar being childless moved and brought the boy
at home and handed over to his wife,
Both the couple accepted Hafiz as their dear one.

The great Allah had answered to her call
the woman bowed and sought blessings in dargah
after a few days she was blessed with a child
she expressed her all devotion to the Almighty.

With great joy she titivated the son,
'It appears, the lord has not forgotten me
and now I am a mother of my own baby.'

'Go to your father', told the mother to Hafiz,
'tell him about the child and convey my salam'.

Gently Hafiz left the home and reached
the city of chittagong with a happy heart
With all regards, Hafiz stood before,
the Subedar became surprised and
asked him the welfare of the home.
- 'Listen to me, my father,' Hafiz replied,
  my mother has given birth to a child.
  I have come here with this tiding
  you are required to go home immediately
- this is my mother's humble submission'.

Listening to this Subedar called the Moulavi
and prayed to the gracious all mighty.
With joy he offered wealth in abundance
and shared his happiness with the sepoys.

There at home, the mother took the child
in her breast and set upon fun and marry making,
she made a long robe for the baby
with great care and affection.

[Oh, the ordeal of Allah is befalling us.]

Saluting the sahib, Hafiz returned home
Subedar then sat together with his sepoys
- 'Listen to me, my sons,

what do I need all the money for?
- I desire to celebrate the birth of the baby
by performing the special prayer'.

There after he offered money in the name ofAllah
the sepoys then came forward and assembled.
the Subeder declared a grand feast
the commander and the sepoys agreed
to go to the market nearby the port.
The Sahib cautioned them not to go far for purchase
and asked to bring fourteen cows unfirtile
along with fourteen caldron to contain the meat
and also hire fourteen cooks.
'I shall bear all the expense' – with that words
the Subedar gave the money to the commander.
Returning home they assembled in the mosque
and sat to fix the day of the celebration.

The fifth day of the week being the auspicious
all were called upon to join the feast
after the day's prayer.
Hafiz invited all,
all the muslims resided in the city.

'Listen ye all, listen to me with all attention,
all will be entertained with on the occasion'.
The Muslims of Chittagong after invitation
all looked forward to join after Friday's prayer.

[Oh! the ordeal of Allah is befalling us.]

On the end of the day of Brihaspati
the cows were sacrificed with sanctity

all the fleshes were stored in the kitchen
and the cooking started on
the following morning.
Lest others would mind
the Subedar bahadur sat for prayer
before lying the caldron on the oven
then the cooking started.

The delicious food had spread the smell
everywhere in the city,
the sepoys rushed towards the spot
to join the assembly.

The smell even reached the nostril of
the Junior English Sahib in his slumber,
waking up from the bed he came out
and was surprised.

[Oh! the day ends with the ordeals of Allah
over the warring sepoys.
Go ye all, recite Koran with all your heart.]

Oh Allah, the ominous circle engulfs us
we hold on to the gracious Muhammad
and now shall proceed on
in our story of the Sahib and the warriors.

'Hark now, my men, I ask you
wherefrom comes the smell of delicate food
coming in the Bungalow'.
The servants were afraid of
speaking the truth,

being assured,
one of them opened his mouth:

'The Subedar is blessed with a son,
today they are performing *akika* of the baby.
They *sacrificed* fourteen cows
with religious rites,
to offer feast to all the Muslims in Chittagong,
after the prayer today they are going to dine.'
Upon this, the Sahib spoke thus:
'Bring my horse immediately
let me go to Subedar's place.
I shall fetch my share and have my fill,
and will see how dare they are'.

'No my master, do not go now,
Feast will start after the prayer
we shall also attend the feast and I assure you
we shall bring your share right here.'

'Go, get my horse ready,
I'm determined to go, come what may.'
Having ascended on the pony
the sahib became furious
and made his move in the name of Jesus.
The servants apprehended
that might be his last move.

With gentle gallop the sahib reached
the cooking shed,
and demanded a pot of meat.
'No, my master, you can't have now,

It is not the right time to get it.

If you come after mid day prayer
We will serve the meat
Or even your share will be sent
With your servant.'

'Give my share right now, I repeat again',
The meat being denied, the anger of the sahib
Knew no bound.
Ascending upon the pony
The sahib charged on the cooks
And plundered on the caldron.

Oh! a day of ordeal comes near
I importune you to recite the Koran
In devout spirit.

[Oh! the ordeal of Allah is befalling us.]
Those who were inside the kitchen shed
With humble submission they
Appeared before the Subedar and said:
'Look, the Sahib had spoilt all the meal
Contained in caldron fourteen.
We tried to dissuade him but
The swain Christian did not listen to it
He spoilt all the dainty meat.'
The hapless Subedar prayed to Allah
He might forgive the mischief
These stuffs are now unholy
for the guests.
But we have vowed these to Allah,

Don't throw the spoils in water
Lest fishes will die,
Don't leave them on earth
These are debased by the English.
Bury them inside the ground
Hence Almighty will forgive the sin.
Go prepare sweetmeats afresh
And entertain all the guests.

The Subedar now arranged
Caldron fourteen
Meanwhile the massage of atrocity,
Reached across the islands.
After midday prayer all the Muslims
Attended the ceremony and
Feasted on the sweets.
Everybody took the share
And made for their own
But who would carry the sweets
For the hostess at home.
'Come forward', asked the Subedar,
'Go one among you,
tell her, all edibles exhausted
all the people attended
these are the last remains'.
But nobody dared to face the mother
With the sweets instead of meat,
At last one old fellow volunteered
To proceed with the sweets.

There in the house of the subedar
The lady was waiting in hunger
And sat with the baby on her lap.
The bearer then appeared with the packet.
She gently placed her son on the bed
In joyful mood opened the covering
And became frustrated.
'Tell me, hey soldier,
don't hide anything
I want to know, why these sweets?
Where has gone all the edibles and the meat.
'Tell me the truth,
or I shall put you to death
you have no reason to fear
tell me, what happened at the feast.'

'It's not wise to avoid you',
replied gently the old man,
'It is the English sahib,
Who debased the sanctity
And spoilt all the delicious plates.

The mother, enraged at it and roared,
'Go, and tell the Subedar that
His first duty is to protect the sanctity.
Let him stay in disgrace with his men.
I' m going to charge the sahib
And slaughter him, come what may.

'Come my baby, feed yourself on my breast
and go to sleep,

Soon I shall be back
from the bungalow of the sahib.

She furnished herself
With war attire and armaments.
She landed on the bungalow of the sahib
Her sword flushed like emerald,
Holding the shield in the left hand
She proceeded towards him.

Breaking seven doors she entered
The inner chamber where
The Sahib was sleeping
With a blanket on his body.
Breaking through the doors seven
She made her way to
Where the Sahib was fast asleep.
'Wake up, hey Christian - born
Having spoiled the sacred feast
Of the Muslims,
How peacefully he sleeps!

'I'll see how mighty you are
In power and wealth
You swain, the coward
Take your sword in both the hands.'

The mother raised her bare sword
Inviting the Christian to a combat
The English Sahib then begged mercy
And bowed down at her feet —
'My mother,forgive me as your own son,

I shall make amends of all my wrong.

'Had it been my own son', replied She,
'Or any Muslim born,
he would not have spoilt the sacred dish
In the city of Chittagong.'

The woman handed him sword three times,
And three times, the infidel refused it.
-'Be witness to it, the Sun and the Moon in the sky,
Be witness Oh, Lord, the unknown, unseen'.

In the name of Holy Allah
She raised her sword
And cut off the head
With a stroke.
Then she sized the body in pieces seven
Like pieces of caught- fish
And wrapped them with a blanket
Keeping it there in the bed
She came back home.

Chanting the name of Allah,
With faith unflinching in Mohammed,
I shall now relate the new phase of the struggle
Between the Sahib and the Sepoys.

The ominous day dawns,
The ordeal of Allah on the Sepoys,
Hold fast on the Holy Koran.

[Oh, the ordeal of Allah befalling us]

Now the beautiful woman met a Sepoy-
'Do not divulge it to the Subedar-
Five of you get ready to go with me
We shall devastate the city of Chittagong.
Put on your attaire soon.

'Be assured, if you die, and be a martyr
For the cause of faith,
It is the blessings of the gracious almighty
A seat in the Heaven is yours.
The men at-arms then proceeded fast,
While the woman remained at home.

Oh Soldiers, listen, the Subedar
Had already got the tidings
Who opened the armoury
And plundered arms and ammunitions.
'Go you all, take your arms
We shall fall upon Chittagong,
The infidels are well trained
In all the mischievous deeds.
The Sahib being in great fear had
Sent messages to the lord in England,
The rebel infantry made massacre in Chittagong.
The English in Bartupi were alarmed at it,

They dispatched a company
Ten thousand by the ships.

The Sepoys in fifteen thousand
Put up resistance
In Chittagong field,

The mother still undaunted
In her determination and spirit.

In the name of Allah,
now We shall proceed on in our recital
Of the tale of the rebellious force.

[Oh, the ordeal of Allah is befalling us.]

'Wake up my sons, wake up and
Take arms in your hands,
The muslims are in great danger
In the tyranny of the infidels.
Ride on the horseback and
Proceed towards the war field
The Almighty is gracious
The enemy will have a lesson.
The brave lady heralded her men
In the name of Allah,
Her clarion call assembled all the
Sepoys of the five battalion.

The mother in the right
The Subedar in the left
The soldiers in the middle -
It is as if the Heaven
Tumbles down on the ocean.

The warriors fell upon
The enemies and cut them into pieces,
Leaving only one infidel alive
To report the messages.

The Christian swains knew the tricks
And sent urgent telegram to England:
Situation critical
Don't waste at Bartupi
Send troops immediately
To rescue Chittagong.
The Subedar revolted
And occupied the city.

On receiving the message
Forty thousand marched forward
While they arrived on the shore
The mother fortified her force
And made aware of the situation.
The five commanders came out
With their troops,
Those who had their food and drink
And those who had not,
All of them now marched forward
At her clarion call.

They fought seven deadly wars
Thirty five thousand soldier fell,
The brave woman killed horses
And their riders too
All the thirty five thousand,
And put an end to the war
In the wink of an eye.

Coming over to her own
The brave mother began to

Shed tears for
The loss of her sons
In the field of war, -

'Oh here me, the warriors all,
Do not be sad over the incidents of Chittagong,
I would not be sorry to die
If it is the will of the God.

The English commander sent messages
And urged for adequate protection,
'They are sure to slaughter me
in the bungalow of Chittagong'.
Forty thousand soldiers were sent
Who made a desperate stride in the battle field,
The woman had an ominous dream
And cried out in her sleep.
She made the prayer and came out
In the name of Allah
Whistled the bugle
And called her followers
To march towards the field.

Herself on the right and Subedar on the left
The woman proceeded
With soldiers and the horses.
The enemies were plundered
In the battle field
Hundreds of them were beheaded
And very few among them remained alive.
The urgent message again sent to England

Seeking military force numbering forty thousand,
The Chittagong would be gone.
Only one has escaped in the bungalow
And the rest are in the field of Rangtuli.

The woman proceeded again with strong force:
'Come forward, ye all Muslims, I call you all,
we shall proceed forwards to embrace martyrdom.
The warriors all gathered in
The field listening to the clarion call
The Five- Commanders came along
Mounted on the horse back
The woman and the Subedar
Flung on the war field.
Seeing the enemy in the front
The mother roared and cried –
'Rise, the believers of Islam
And join us to sacrifice your lives
For the religion, come what may
Slay the Firingis
It is the day.

In the name of Allah, she raised her whip
The horses jumped on the battlefield
There's no measure who killed whom –
Forty five thousand against
Ten thousand insurgents.
She slaughtered the enemies all
Being a single man to report the matter.
When she returned from the field,

The mother counted her sons and
Discovered, two were missing.

'Listen, oh warriors, my sons,
we have had enough,
we must leave now.
Please look for two of my sons
Who have lost their life in the war of Kharbojar.

Having buried the two warriors,
They went to their house.
It's at that, the royal treasury
Was flung open,
Open to all to snatch whatever they want.
'We must fly away the land
Get ready, my sons,
Take whatever you can.

Horses and men have crossed the river swimming,
Those who could, used the caldron as canopy
Even sacred fur carried them
To over come the catastrophe.
With their kith and keen all the warriors
Led by the mother and the Subedar
Abandoned the city of Chittagong.

They arrived at the highway
With the desire to reach the hills of Jayantia
If Allah blessed them.
They proceeded in lines
While passersby flew away in fear

One old man dared to ask them -
Who they were, where they were going.

'Oh, ask no question on it,
we salute you, accept our greetings.
we do not know where our destiny is,
we do not know who would
provide us food and shelter.
We only know we have abandoned Chittagong
Only the Almighty knows,
where He would lead us to.

When they had reached a distant place
The fatigued sepoys were unable to move
Found a deep forest in front
They took their shelter there.
A fisherman who was
Rabai Patni by name
Was passing with his net
Nearby a stream.
Finding them in the dense forest
He came forward and stood before
'Who are you ', asked Rabai,
'which way to go?
where are you from?
Tell me frankly all the details
Ye the strangers.

'We 're Muslims, we 've escaped from
The city of Chittagong,
Please help us, for the English savages

Chasing us from behind.
Would you please, show us
The path to Jayantia,
We could then be saved,
And this great service of yours
Would be blessed by the Almighty.

Rabai then with his net
Mounted on the hill-road,
He found from a distance that
The infidels had already arrived
In search of the sepoys.

While the sahib enquired
About the absconders,
Rabai replied with all simplicity,
'Yes, sir, I have found them proceeding
Towards the east,
They are sure to cross the hill on horseback
Before you could trace.

The troops then in their search
proceeded forthwith following false path
While Rabai came back to fish in the stream.
Returning home Rabai had
Sent his five sons to prepare food
He then brought cows and goats
And had arranged a grand feast.

He appeared before the Subedar
And the mother with solemn greetings
And narrated the incident of the meeting.

'Listen, my mother, I tell you the truth,
I have sent the English soldiers towards
The east who are in seared of you.

While keeping you here
Inside the wild forest,
I have sent them over there
To cross the mountain.
While they have proceed the other side
I now invite you to dine at my place.

In the humble cottage of Rabai
There lived five sons, three with their wives,
All were engaged in preparation of the feast.
Food was cooked in abundance
And then they said their prayers,

With them joined Rabai and his five sons too
who were converted to Islam.
On that occasion
Along with Rabai all the fishermen of the place
Embraced the new faith, and dined.
Rabai prayed to the virtuous sepoys
To leave one of them for their initiation
Into the new belief and order.

The woman left one amongst her men
They built a mosque and trained
Rabai in the Islamic cult,

'Hey there, I declared it before you
Never call him Rabai Patni anymore,
He is now Rabai Morol, the leader.

Now the warriors finish their feast
And prayed to Rabai to show
The path to Langla city.

'Go you through the western bank of the lake
You will soon reach there.
Do not be afraid,
there is Ali Amjad
you may seek shelter.

At the call of the woman
The soldiers all mounted on the horse
In the name of Allah,
The five warriors made for their journey
Next day morning they arrived
At the town of Langla.

'Who is the lord of the land, show us the way
To the zamindar of Langla.
An old man answered them thus:
'Zamindar Ali Amjad sahib is a great
There is no one like him in the whole of Sylhet.

Hearing this the warriors became happy
And appeared before the outhouse
Looking at the soldiers in the early morning
The people began to murmur.
Hearing this Ali Amjad came out of his room
And asked,
'How come, all these soldiers here!
Subedar came forward and offered his salam
Narrated the whole story,

Gave a patient hearing to the tale
Ali Amjad then arranged a great feast
With cows and goats and provided shelter.
When the food was about to be ready
There reached the enemy in their search.

The soldiers knew, they had to go without food,
All of them had withdrawn from the house.
The marketplace was made wide open
The soldiers might take whatever they willed
The Zamindar would pay for it.
Having looted the market of Ali Amjad
The soldiers gone their own way remembering Allah.
The soldiers all thus escaped from Langla
Rushed through the hills nearby
And reached Kulaura.

They were all tired and
Incapable of bearing the strains.
Hungry as they were all
They plundered the orchards
To satisfy their hunger.
And left double the amount
Of whatever they took as compensation.
This way they moved for three days
And at the end of the day
They touched upon Khan Bahadurpur.

They came across an old man
On the way and asked:
'Tell us, my father, who's the

Zamindar of the place
We wish to go to his house.'
-'Oh, look, there stands his
Beautiful house over there.
Having reached the Zamindar's place
They prayed for food and shelter.
- 'We have left our house,
we've left our all resort.
We are all Muslims
We beg with the belief that
Being a Muslim, your kindness
Will provide us with all helps.

The Zamindar Nabab Mian brought
Cows and goats to entertain them
After a long days the hungry warriors
Feasted properly there
And thanked God for his blessing.

Oh lord, be with us and lead the
Soldiers towards your path
For none but Allah exists for us.

With a pleasant heart
The soldiers are now on their way to Latu- bazar.
When they came near the town, they met
An old man on the road side.
'Tell us, my father, which place is this.'
Asked the Subedar,
'You're in Latu gaon.'

- 'What a surprise! leaving behind

the Chittagong, we 're here at Latu.'
All the soldiers cheered -
'Oh father, tell us who is the
Zamindar here, we wish to meet him.'

- 'Kalamia is the zamindar of this land
No one is powerful in Latu to him'.

- 'We wish to go to his house
Please show us the way'.

Guided by the old man
The warriors reached there
And slowly entered into the outhouse.
Subedar and his wife then stood before
Kalamia and calmly told,
- 'Listen to us, we brief you,
We're travelers from distant land,
Please offer us some food for the present
And show us the way towards Jayantia.

'Where you come from, if I may ask you,
Where do you wish to go?

- 'We're from Chittagong, earned the wrath
Of Christian, they are all strange bad fellows,
Knowing hundreds of tricks.
As a Muslim, please help us,
And if God wills it, we shall ascend the
Hill of Jayantia.'

In the name of Allah, depending on
Mohammad, we shall proceed on our
Account of the *Jangiyas*.

The ordeal of Allah on the warriors,
Be prepared for it,
Fortified with the Holy Koran
Oh, ye all my sons.

Having called upon his five sons,
Kalamia ordered them to arrange
A great feast for the warriors
With cow and goats' meat.
Himself prepared to go out.

- 'Oh, my father, where are you going,
  We come to seek your help.

- 'Do not be worried, my sons are here
To look after your needs.

Kalamia then came out of his house
And looked towards *Muria haoar*
And saw a number of Christian soldiers
Who came forward to converse.

- 'Have you seen the warriors here around?
  'What will be my reward, if I
  tell you the truth?

- 'Oh, be assured, we promise you
  The lordship of this place,
  The market of Latu will be yours.

- 'Do come here crossing the river
I assure you hundred rupees,
Take a small boat and come near.'

Here the woman had an ominous dream

Kalamia was going to inform the Christian
With an evil design.
She called upon the subedar
To get ready for departure.

- 'The food of this place in not for us.
  Come, my sons all, we are not
  Going to stay here any more.
  She gave the clarion call
  And thus became ready
  All the five warrior sons,

The enemy too, reached the place
Right at the moment.

- 'Oh, Allah, punish this wicked fellow
  Kalamia, the betrayer,
  I seek redressal for it,'
  -the mother made the prayer.

Suddenly a terrible storm raised
Plundering the villages and town of Latu.
A big mango tree fell on the house
Killing two sons (of Kalamia) .
The Christian soldiers all
Had fled away fearing the storm.
The mother was thirsty
She at once rushed
And reached Malegarah hill
With all her soldiers.

The drops of water she drank
could not quench her thirst,

Unknowingly she raised
The last cup in her lip,
And the destined fate
dragged her towards the river.
She remembered the seven wars in Chittagong,
She remembered her child and then

The thirsty mother opened the haversack
Wherein the baby was tied up on her back.

- 'Oh! he has passed away unaware and
Turned into a stiff mass of flesh.'
With the decomposed baby in her arms
The mother burst into tears.

[Oh, the ordered of Allah is befalling us]

All the warriors started wailing,
And performed the last rites
Subedar tried to console them,
- 'The homeless destitute we are thy all.
- It's our fate, and we have
No control over it, just to be accepted.
Who can tell, when shall I breath my last!
Bury the dead after taking bath.
It is the wish of the Almighty
To perform the duty on the earth.

'The mother too has left us alone,
Breaking away with all the terrestrial
bondage.'
Nobody could see how
One evil Christian kept hidden

Under the bamboo bush;

How he fired a bullet
Through her breast,
While she was
Cleaning herself on the river water in sacred way,
And wished to have a gulp of water
To quench her thirst.

The dirty Christian took that
Opportunity to strike at her.
When the scream was heard
The warriors made a loud uproar.
But nowhere the assailant could be
traced.
They tried to carry her to Malegareh
But the Almighty had done with her
Before they could reach there.

[Oh! The ordeal of Allah is befalling us.]

The warrior- mother breathed her last
At a very desperate moment,
Who knows the ways of God.
The warriors all began to cry aloud,
They were all rendered motherless
In the land of Latu.

'They had her washed
With great care,
Decked her with new clothes,
Had the sweet smelling perfume
Strewn on her body, scented powder

Rubbed on her forehead,
They dug her grave.

Whoever wishes may go
To *Malegarah mokam,*
He will find two graves
One of the wretched sons,
The other of the warrior-mother,
They are lying there
Unknown to the world outside
Forever.

Having buried the warrior-woman
The followers now mounted upon
The Hill of Malegarh.
They had no arms
No ammunition, how could they
Fight against the Christian!
The Firangis on the other side
Throwing gun shot incessantly,
With no arms to encounter,
They picked up bricks and stone chips.

[Oh! The ordeal of Allah is befalling us]

The warriors realized
It was the act of Kalamia,
Who created obstacles
To make their movement slow,
Now the warriors put sand
On the gun to shot fire
Killing the Christians in large number.

Kalamia did all the mischief
Against the warriors,
The warriors fought bravely
In vain,to overcome
All the barriers.
Seventeen among them
Were arrested by the Christians at last
The Firangis were happy to make the capture.
They tied them in the trees
And shoot at them mercilessly.
The more they shot, the more indomitable
They became.
Then spoke the warriors:
'you cannot put an end to us
this way, hey Christians,
Set us free, to have us a bath in the
River and
Allow us to say our prayer.'

The Christian acted likewise.
The warriors were allowed
To have a dip in the river
With handcuff in their hands.
Having washed themselves
The warriors said their prayer
In sacred way following the
Dictates of the Holy Koran.
They were all devout Muslims
And prayed to Aliah to
Lead them in their last ride.

[Oh! the ordeal of Allah is befalling us]

Thereafter, the warriors
stood in a line under the fateful tree.
They were given new dresses,
The sacred Koran was removed from them.
They had their last prayer
And thus prepared to die.

-'Hear me, oh my fellow brethren
In the infidel's troop
We urge upon you to fight,
For the cause of religion.
Come, ye, Christian gunmen
Drop your arms, and take up
Guns from our hand.
Kill us with our guns
Shot us at a time,
And this done, we shall be killed
And we shall attain martyrdom'.

Having said the last prayer
The seventeen soldiers prepared for
The last hour.
Having received the gun-shot
The warriors fell upon the ground
Facing the sacred western direction
The seventeen of them counted martyrdom
I bring this tiding before you.

Oh, the warriors
The Jangiyas bewail

In their tryst,
Feeding on the wild grass;
The Subedar bahadur, again, bewail
For the Holy faith.
Leaving aside Latu
They marched forward,
And there after landed
In the village Patu.

[Oh, the Jangiyas bewail
In their tryst,
Feeding on the wild grass.]

Reaching the village Patu,
The Jangiyas began to feed
On leaves of the gardens.
While eating the leaves of vegetables
They leave money on the creepers
To compensate for the loss.
Leaving aside this village
They marched forward
And thereafter landed in the village Barapara.

[Oh, the Jangiyas bewail...]

The Jangiyas bewail
In their tryst,
Feeding on the wild grass.

The warriors satisfy their hunger
In Barapara,
They picked up leaves of reddish.
And having chewed the vegitables

In their terrible plight
They rushed towards
The village Bedrong
with tears in their eyes.

The warriors all,
Landed thereafter
In the village called Maizgram,
There they had their fill with
The juice of the sugarcane.

[Oh! the Jangiyas bewail...]

Having crossed Maizgram
They came upon a village called Bishkut
An old man there was cutting wood.
- 'Tell us hey, wood cutter,
  who is the lord of the village? '
  'Hey strangers you,
  I'm afraid to tell you'
- 'Fear no more, we are warriors
  retreating from the field.'
  'Now take it from me, the zamindar is
  very rich man here,
  he is called Suruzmia by name.
  Go forward this way, you'll find his house
  Very soon.

[Oh! Allah, the Jangiyas bewail...]

When they reached the house of
Suruzmia Choudhury
He was in the out-house

They exchanged salam
And began to converse,
-'Please, we shall ask for a meal of you
we're hungry.

- 'Oh no, I have nothing to offer to you.'
- 'Why don't you then show us the
way to Bishkut,
We wish to proceed towards Jayantia
We are confused.

[Oh, Allah, the Jangiyas bewail.]

'You 're from Chittagong,
crossing only one *kut* distance'.
Suruzmia dissuaded them,
'Go nineteen *kut* further
You shall reach Bishkut then'.
The warriors were dumbfounded
Hearing it.
They were really in a fix.
Oh, Allah, the Jangiyas bewail,
the day has come to an end
the ordeal of Allah on the warriors,
hold fast on to the Holly Koran...

The hungry warriors now crossed Bishkut
And landed on Anair haor,
They are tired beyond measure
And incapable of moving a step further.
[Oh, Allah, the Jangiyas bewail.]

They walked through the Anair haor

and entered into the field of grains,
They picked up leaves of linseeds
and had their fill with it.

They scattered money in the field
Compensating the loss of the peasants
and rushed forward to escape the enemy.

[Oh, Allah, the Jangiyas bewail...]

Having crossed the Anair haor
They landed on the forest of Fazia khan,
An old man with a fishing rod.
'Oh my father, tell us now
Where, who is the landlord.?

'He's millionaire, named Golam Rabbani,
there is none else to equal him
in the entire region of Badarpur.'
Hearing this the warriors made for
The house of the Zamindar.
[Oh Allah, the Jangiyas bewil.]
Golam Rabbani was on his way to the pond
On the way they met him
And exchanged salam,
And the warriors spoke to him
All in details:

- 'We're from Chittagong, retreating
  from the battle.
  'We wish to go to the Hills of Jayantia
  We're hungry incapable to move any more.

In the name of Allah,
Please provide us with food and shelter.'

'Hold on now, I'm going to feed you with
my humble lot,
Almighty is gracious
come to my home.'
The out-house was made open,
Cordial hospitality extended to them.
They stayed one night and resolved
Not to waste time there
Enemy is all around,
Who knows, the way the infidels
Might attack.

- 'Please show us the way towards Jayantia
and let us proceed there soon.'

- 'Go ahead, there is a river nearby
cross it, my son,
you will find Jayantia hill in your front.
With gloomy heart
The Jangiyas took their path
And landed near Badarpur,
The Christian, meantime,
got the information.
The fugitive troops were
On their way to Jayantia kindom.

With no arms, no ammunitions
How could they fight.
Lumps of earth they put

Inside the guns and made shots
And they in the name of Allah
Stroke on their own breast.
They raised hue and cry
And combated the enemy in vain.
Oh, what a horror it is
Subedar received the bullet.

[Oh! the Jangiyas bewail.]

The warriors fled away into the
Hill range of Badarpur,
No one could tell where
they had gone and taken shelter.
The Subedar breathed his last at Badarpur hill
No one could trace his body
None could say any more.

[Oh, the Jangiyas bewail.]

I offer my salam to five Messengers of Allah
I offer my salam to my Muslim brethren,
My salam to the master who instructed
To relate this tale of the warriors.
I present this story with all my passion
Forgive my incompability.
Forgive me for the wrongs
That I might have committed
In narrating this tale of
The war of the *Jangiyas*,
To you all, unwillingly.

NORTH EAST INDIA

The Route Followed by the Mutineers..........

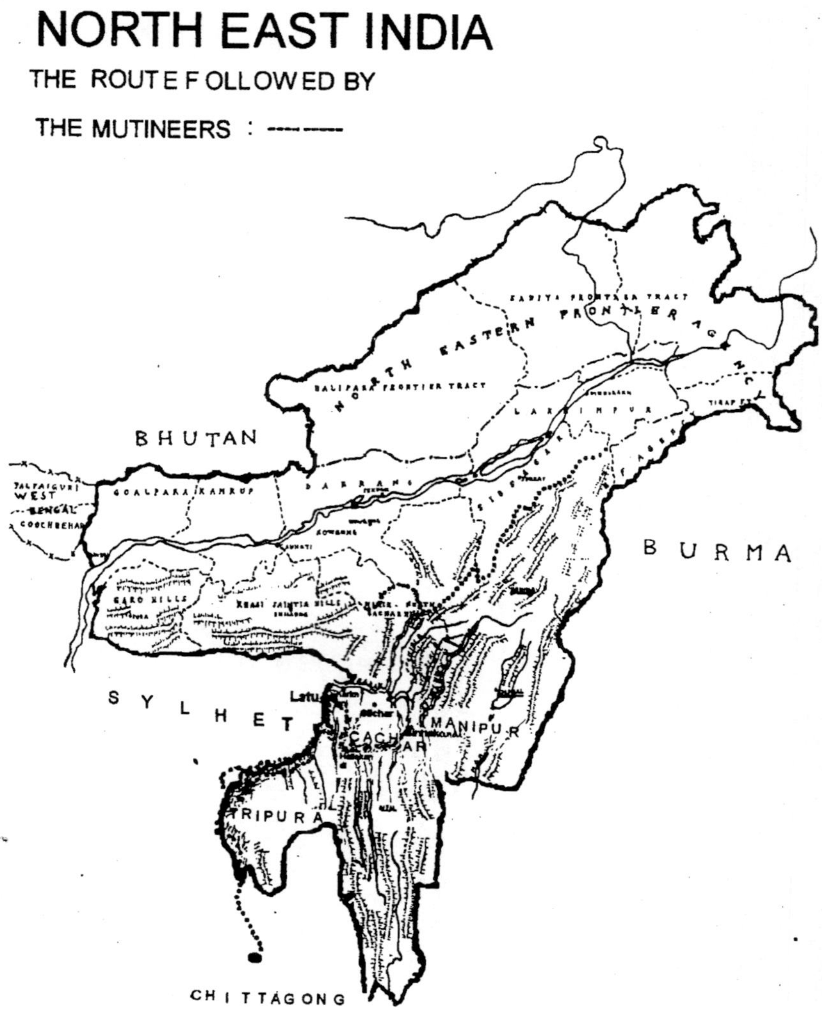

NORTH EAST INDIA

The Route Followed by the Mutineers..........

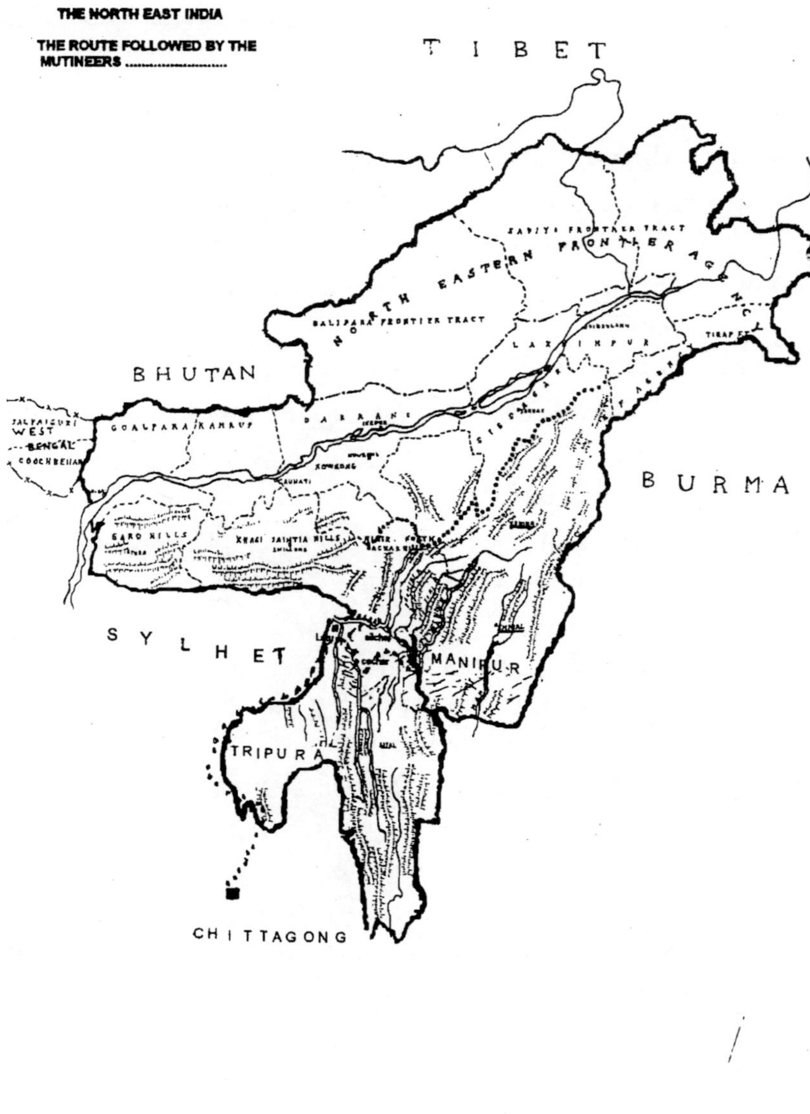

Bibliography

English Books

Akhtar, Sirin: *The Role of Zamindar in Bengal (1707-1772)*. Asiatic Society of Bangladesh, Dacca, 1982.

Ahmed, Qeyam Uddin: *The Wahabi Movement in India*, Calcutta, 1966.

Allen, B.C.: *Assam District Gazetteers*, Shillong, 1906.

Allen, B.C.: *Eastern Bengal District Gazetteers*, Dacca, 1912.

Banerjee, A.C.: *The Eastern Frontier of British India*, Calcutta, 1946.

Barpujari, H.K.: *Assam in the Days of Company (1826-1858)*, Gauhati, 1980.

Becker, C.: *History of the Catholic Missions in North East India 1890 – 1915*, (first German edition, 1923), edited and translated by G. Stadler and S. Karotemprel, Shillong, 1980.

Bhattacharjee, J.B.: *Cachar under British Rule in North East India*, New Delhi, 1977.

Bhuyan, S.K.: *Early British Relations with Assam*, Shillong, 1928.

Bhuian, S.K.: *Anglo Assamese Relations, 1771 – 1826*, Gauhati, 1949.

Bradley-Birt (F.B.): *Sylhet - Thackery*, London, 1911.

Buckland, C.E.: *Bengal under Lieutenant Governors*, Vol. I – II, Calcutta, 1901.

Chakravarty, B.P.: *Annexation of Cachar* (1832), proceedings, Indian Historical Records Commission, 1942.

Chakravorty, Birendra Chandra: *British Relations with the Hill Tribes of Assam Since 1858*, Calcutta, 1981.

Choudhury, Sujit (ed.): *The Mutiny Period in Cachar*, Silchar, 1981.

Chattarjee, Suniti Kumar: *Origin and Development of the Bangali Language*, Vol. I-II, Calcutta, 1926.

Dalton, E.T.: *Descriptive Ethnology of Bengal*, reprint, Calcutta, 1973.

Das Gupta, Sashi Bhusan: *Obscure Religious Cults*, Calcutta, 1976.

Datta, Debabrata (ed.): *Cachar District Records*, Silchar, 1969.

Dutta, K.N.: *Landmarks of the Freedom Struggle in Assam*, Gauhati, 1958.

Datta, Kalikinkar: *Reflections on the Mutiny*, C.U., 1967.

Embre, Ainslie T.: *1857 in India: Mutiny or War of Independence*, Boston.

Gait, Edward: *A History of Assam*, second edition, Gauhati, 1962.

Ghosh, Jamini Mohan: *Sannyasi Fakir Raiders of Bengal*, Calcutta, 1930.

Goswami, Prafulladatta: *Bihu Songs of Assam*, Gauhati, 1957.

Grierson, G.A.: *Linguistic Survey of India*, Vol. V, Part I, Calcutta, 1903.

Guha, Amalendu: Impact of Bengal Renaissance on Assam, *Journal of the Indian Economic and Social History Review*, 1968.

Hamilton, F.: *An Account of Assam*, first compiled in 1807 – 1814., Edited by S.K. Bhuiyan, Gauhati, 1940.

Haque, Anwarul: *Mahimals — the Muslim Fishermen Community of Barak Valley, Assam*. Karimganj, 1984.

Hunter, W.W.: *A Statistical Account of Bengal*, London, 1876.

Hunter, W.W.: *Statistical Accounts of Assam,* Vol. II (Sylhet), 1926.

Hunter, W.W: *The Indian Mussalmans*, Dacca, Bangladesh, 1975.

Hunter, W.W.: *Imperial Gazetteer of India,* Vol. II, 1881.

Joshi, Puran Chand.: *1857 in Folk Songs*, (Compiled & Edited.) New Delhi, 1994.

Karl Marx and F. Engels: *The First Indian War of Independence*, *1857-59,* (Moscow, Foreign Languages Publishing House, 2nd Imprint).

Khan, Sarafraj.: *The Forgotten Mass Movement of Bengal in the Eighteenth Century*, Dacca, 1970.

Kaye, J.E.: *History of the Sepoy War in India, 1857 – 1858*, Vol. I –III., London, 1877-1878.

Schueking L.L.: *The Sociology of Literary Tests*; London, 1948.

Lahiri, R.M.: *Annexation of Assam*, Calcutta, 1954.

Leonard, A. Gordon.: *Bengal: The Nationalist Movement, 1876 – 1940*, London, 1974.

Lowe, Charles, Rath Bone: *History of the Indian Navy, 1613-1863* London, 1877.

Mackenzie, Alexander: *The North East Frontier of India,* New Delhi, 1999.

Mazumdar, Hriday Nath: *Reminiscences of Dacca.,* Dacca, 1926.

Majumdar, R.C.: *Sepoy Mutiny and the Revolt of 1857,* Calcutta, 1957, (Second edition, 1963).

Majumdar, Geeta: *Folk Tale of India Series: Folk-tales of Bengal*, New Delhi, 1978.

Mukharjee, Hiren: *India's Struggle for Freedom,* Calcutta, 1958.

Mukharjee, Nilmani: *A Bengal Zamindar Joy Krishna Mukharjee of Uttarpara and His Times (1808-1838),* Calcutta, 1975.

Nath, Raj Mohan: *The Background of Assamese Culture*, Shillong, 1986.

Nath, Raj Mohan: *Antiquities of Cachar*, Silchar, 1981.

Paul, Bipin Chandra: *Story of My Life and Times* [Vol.I, 1858-1885., Vol, II., 1886 – 1900], Calcutta, 1936.

Paul, Bipin Chandra: *Memoirs of My Life and Time*, Calcutta, 1952.

Pemberton, R.B.: *Report on the Eastern Frontier of British India,* Second Impression, Gauhati, 1966.

Pianazzi, A.: *In the Garo Land,* Calcutta, 1935.

Qureshi, Prof. Basir Ahmed: *Standard Twentieth Century Dictionary: Urdu into English*, Delhi, 1981.

Richard, N. Dorson (ed.): *Introductions–Folklores and Traditional History*, New York, 1973.

Roy, Sambhucharan: *History of Sylhet,* Sylhet, 1875.

Seal, Anil: *The Emergence of Indian Nationalism*, Cambridge, University Press, 1971.

Sen, Dinesh Chandra: *Eastern Bengal Ballads,* Calcutta, 1923.

Sen, Surendra Nath: *Eighteen Fifty Seven*, New Delhi, 1958.

Soppit, C.A.: *A Historical and Descriptive Account of the Kachari Tribes in the North Cachar Hills*, Shillong, 1885.

Tarachand.: *History of the Freedom Movement in India*, Vol. II, New Delhi, 1967.

Zevital, Dr. Susan: *Bengali Folk- Ballads from Mymensing and the Problem of their Authenticity*, University of Calcutta, 1963.

Accounts, Journals, Records, Memoirs etc.

Allen, B.C.: *Sylhet District Gazetteer*, Shillong, 1905. *The Gazetteer of Cachar*, Shillong, 1905.

Assam Proceedings, belonging to the Bengal Government: Government of India, and the Assam Government, 1858 – 1900.

Judicial Proceedings, 1858-1900, National Archives, New Delhi.

Bengal Judicial Proceedings, 1857-1862, State Archives, Govt. of West Bengal, Calcutta.

Bengal Judicial Proceedings, July 29, 1858. No. 115; *Holroyd to Young, June, 28.*

Buchanan-Hamilton, Francis: *An Account of Assam, 1807-14,* Gauhati, 1963.

Butler, J: *Travels and Adventures in the Province of Assam*, London, 1855.

Datta, Debabrata: *Cachar District Records*, Silchar, 1969.

Dewan, Maniram, Native Account of Washing Gold in Assam, *Journal of the Asiatic Society of Bengal,* VIII, 1838.

Fisher, T., Captain.: *Memoir of the Countries on and Near the Eastern Frontier of Sylhet.*

Friend of India, Feb. 9, 1858.

Hindu Patriot, August 20, 1857, August 22, 1860.

Jenkins, H.L.: *Note on the Burmese route from Assam to Hookoong Valley,* Proceedings, Asiatic Society, Bengal.

Mishra, Bani Prassanna: Occassional paper –1: 'The Sannyasi Rebellion — The Sociology and Economics of A conflict in Sub-Himalayan Bengal, Center For Himalayan Studies, University of North Bengal, June, 1985.

Proceedings of North-East India History Association, Fourth Session, Shillong, 1983.

Sen, Jyotirmoy: *Untold Story of Mutineers in Cachar. Raijor Batory (Peoples' News),* Director of Information Assam, Gauhati, 1975.

The Dacca News, June 19,1858.

The English Men and Military Chronicle, 2nd Feb, 1858.

Wade, J.P: *An Account of Assam (1793-1800),* Edited by Benudhar Sharma Sibsagar, Assam.

Bengali Authors and Books

Ahmed, Md. Kazi: *Srihatta Darpan*, Sylhet, 1885.

Ali, Sayed Murtaza.: *Hazrat Shah Jalal O Sylheter Itihas*, Bangla Academy, Dacca, 1965.

Anisujjaman: *Muslim Manas O Bangla Sahitya*, Dacca, 1963.

Bandyopadhyay, Asit Kumar: *Bangla Sahityer Itibritta*. Kolkata, 1962.

Bandyopadhay, Brajendranath: *Sambad Patre Sekaler Katha*, Kolkata, 1401 B.S.

Bandyopadhyay, Suprasanna: *Itihas Asrita Bangala Kabita*, Calcutta, 1954.

Choudhury, Achyut Charan: *Srihatter Itibritta,* Vol. I, II, Calcutta, 1910, Silchar, 1916.

Choudhury, Dewan Nurul Anwar Hussain: *Jalalabader Katha*, Bangla Academy, Dacca, 1982.

Chakraborty, Ratan Lal: *Sipahee Juddha O Bangladesh*, Dacca, 1984.

Choudhury, Golam Akba: *Loka Sahityer Katha*, Sylhet, 1988.

Dtta, Gurusaday O Bhowmik, Nirmalendu.: *Srihatter Loka Sangit*, Kolkata, 1988.

Devi, Prabhamoyee: *Bangla Akhyaika Kavya*, C.U., 1958.

Ghosh, Binoy: *Bangalar Naba Jagriti*, Kolkata, 1979, B.S.

Ghosh, Binoy.: *Samayik Patre Bangalar Samaj Chitra*, Vol. III, Calcutta, 1964.

Guha, Upendra Chandra: *Cacharer Itibritta*, Dacca, 1921.

Gupta, Narendra Chandra.: *Srihatta Pratibha.*

Gupta, Rajanikanta.: *Sipahi Juddher Itihas*, Vol. I-1V, Calcutta, 1897, 1910.

Kar, Subir: *Achyut Charan Tatwanidhi, Jibani O Sahitya*, Karimganj, 1991.

Kar, Subir: *Srihatter Itibritta*, vol. 1, Guwhati, [ed.] 1402 BS.

Kar, Subir: *Bidrohakal 1857 O Surma- Barak Upatyaka*, Karimganj, 1992.

Kar, Subir.: *Barak Upatyakar Bhasa Sangramer Itihas.* Calcutta, 1999.

Kar, Subir.: *Maha Bidroher Droha gatha – Jangiyar Geet*, [edt.] Calcutta, 2000.

Mirja Nathan: *Baharistan I Ghaybi*, Dacca, 1993.

Mitra, Sukumar: *Unish Shataker Bangla sahitye Bidroher Chitra*. Calcutta, 1960.

Muhammad Manirujjaman: *Adhunik Bangla Kabye Hindu-Musalman Samparka*, Dacca, 1970.

Musa, Kalim: *Madhyajuger Sahitye Hindu-Musalman Samparka.*

Nath, Raj Mohan: *Sonadhaner Geet*, Srihatta Sahitya Parishad, Sylhet, 1947.

Roy, Nihar Ranjan: *Bangalir Itihas*, Calcutta, 1356 B.S.

Roy, Suprakash: *Bharater Krishak Bidroha O Ganatantrik Sangram,* Calcutta, 1972.

Sarma, Chanchal Kumar: *Surma Upatyakar Krishak O Sramik Andolaner Itihas*, Calcutta, 1990.

Shastri, Shib Nath: *Ramtanu Lahiri O Tatkalin Banga-samaj*, Kolkata, 1956.

Sen, Dinesh Chandra: *Banga Bhasa O Sahitya*, Calcutta, 1986.

Sen, Dinesh Chandra: *Brihat Banga*, Kolkata, 1993.

Sen, Satyen: *Mahabidroher Kahini*, Calcutta, 1971.

Sen, Sukumar: *Bangla Sahityer Itihas*, Calcutta, 1991.

Sur, Nikhil: *Chhiyattarer Mannantar O Sannyasi- Fakir Bidroha*. Calcutta, 1974

Umar, Badruddin: *Chirasthayi Bandobasta O Bangladesher Krishak.* Dacca, 1982.

Assamese

Bhuyan, S.K.: *Barphukanar Git*, Gauhati, 1925.

Barua, Maniram: *Buranji Vivek-Ratna,* 1838, Mss. No. 272, Transcript No. 108, Gauhati.

Neog, M.: *Asamiya Sahityer Ruprekha,* Gauhati, 1962.

Sarma, Benudhar: *Maniram Dewan,* Gauhati, 1950. Accounts, Journals and Records etc.

Bengali

Centenary Souvenir, Government Higher Secondary School, Silchar, 1963. *Loka Charyya*, Loka Sanskriti, Guwahati, 1999.

Samachar Darpan, 1857- 62.

Janmat, (Hindi), Barsha 25, Ank 3, Patna, 2007.

Index

Index

■■■